Workbook for *Methods of*

Workbook for *Methods of Macroeconomic Dynamics*

Stephen J. Turnovsky and Michael K. Hendrickson

The MIT Press
Cambridge, Massachusetts
London, England

© 1996 Massachusetts Institute of Technology

All rights reserved. No part of this book may be reproduced in any form by any electronic or mechanical means (including photocopying, recording, or information storage and retrieval) without permission in writing from the publisher.

This book was printed and bound in the United States of America.

ISBN 0-262-70058-1

Contents

Preface		vii
1	Introduction and Overview	1
2	A Dynamic Portfolio Balance Macroeconomic Model	3
3	Rational Expectations: Some Basic Issues	9
4	Rational Expectations and Policy Neutrality	15
5	Nonuniqueness Issues in Rational Expectations Models	21
6	Rational Expectations and Saddlepoint Behavior	29
7	The Stability of Government Deficit Financing under Rational Expectations	43
8	Macroeconomic Stabilization Policy under Rational Expectations	53
9	The Representative Agent Model	65
10	Equilibrium in a Decentralized Economy with Distortionary Taxes and Inflation	77
11	A Dynamic Analysis of Taxes	85
12	The Representative Agent in the International Economy	95
13	An Introduction to Endogenous Growth Models	107
14	Continuous-Time Stochastic Optimization	115
15	A Stochastic Intertemporal Model of a Small Open Economy	123

Preface

We wish to thank a number of individuals, without whom this workbook would not have been possible. First, we based a number of exercises on various published works, which are referenced within the body of the workbook. These authors' contributions to our understanding of the issues and methods explored in *Methods of Macroeconomic Dynamics* are greatly appreciated. Second, we must give credit to Charles Engel and Richard Hartman, whose test questions for graduate courses and comprehensive exams in the University of Washington's Department of Economics were another rich source of exercises for this workbook. In addition, several questions were inspired by Charles Engel's international finance course lectures. Finally, this book would not have been possible without Geri Hendrickson's assistance and encouragement. She typed a significant portion of the manuscript and provided invaluable advice and support.

Workbook for *Methods of Macroeconomic Dynamics*

1 Introduction and Overview

This workbook was written to accompany *Methods of Macroeconomic Dynamics* by Stephen Turnovsky, which we very simply refer to as "the text" throughout the current volume. The purpose of this workbook is to provide students of macroeconomic theory with lots of opportunities to practice the methods that are explained and illustrated in the text. Nobody can learn these methods without diving in and working through problems, and this workbook provides a significant number of them (100, to be exact).

The organization of the current volume mirrors that of the text it accompanies. There are fourteen substantive chapters (2 through 15 in the contents). Two chapters have eight exercises, while there are seven exercises for each of the other twelve chapters. Each exercise is numbered, and includes a hint and solution. You may be able to solve many exercises without reading beyond the question, while other exercises may be unclear until you read the hint. In general, the exercises near the start of the book and the first few exercises in each chapter are the easiest to solve.

As we indicate in the preface, several exercises are based upon published works, which are generally referenced in the text as well as in this workbook. We usually simplify the model, relative to its original presentation in the literature, and use the simplified version as the basis for a few exercises. Our objective is to break the analysis into several manageable steps, with a hint and solution for each portion. If you are unable to solve the first in a related group of exercises, read the solution and attempt to "reverse engineer" it. Then go on with the next exercise in the group. This is the same process by which you might work through the details of a journal article.

You will need a great deal of self motivation to solve the exercises in this workbook (or any significant proportion of them). However, if you persevere, you will be well on your way to mastering some of the basic methods of macroeconomic dynamic analysis. Good luck!

2 A Dynamic Portfolio Balance Macroeconomic Model

Exercise 2.1

Find the general solution to differential equation (2.32) in the text.

Hint: Rewrite (2.32) in the form $\dot{\pi}(t) + \gamma\pi(t) = \gamma p(t)$ and multiply through by the appropriate integrating factor.

Solution: $\pi(t) = \gamma \int p(t)\,dt + ce^{-\gamma t}$, where c is an arbitrary constant.

Exercise 2.2

Derive the formal conditions for system (2.39) in the text to have a stable solution.

Hint: Write down the characteristic equation for the system and use the quadratic theorem to derive expressions for its two roots. Work through each of the following possible cases: zero discriminant, negative discriminant, and positive discriminant.

Solution: The following conditions must be satisfied if (2.39) is to have a stable solution:

$$\gamma\left(\frac{\partial p}{\partial \pi} - 1\right) + (r - p) + A\left(\frac{\partial r}{\partial A} - \frac{\partial p}{\partial A}\right) < 0, \text{ and}$$

$$\gamma \frac{\partial p}{\partial A} A \left(\frac{\partial r}{\partial \pi} - \frac{\partial p}{\partial \pi}\right) > 0.$$

One could substitute the derivative expressions given in Table 2.1A in the text and attempt to simplify the resulting inequalities.

Exercise 2.3

Suppose the benchmark monetary policy for the economy described by equations (2.33) and (2.34) in the text is to maintain a constant ratio of bonds to money. Write down the equations describing the economy in this case, where:

$$\frac{B}{M} = \lambda = \text{a constant}.$$

Hint: Use the following relations to substitute b and m out of the equations:

$$\lambda = \frac{B}{M} = \frac{bP}{mP} = \frac{b}{m}, \text{ and } A = m + b.$$

Solution: The economy is described by the following equations in this case:

$$Y = D\left(Y - T + r\frac{\lambda}{1+\lambda}A - \pi A, r - \pi, A\right) + G,$$

$$A = (1+\lambda)L(Y, r, A),$$

$$p = \alpha(Y - \bar{Y}) + \pi,$$

$$\dot{\pi} = \gamma(p - \pi), \text{ and}$$

$$\dot{A} = G - T + r\frac{\lambda}{1+\lambda}A - pA.$$

Exercise 2.4

Using the static equations you solved for in Exercise 2.3, write down and attempt to sign the expressions for the instantaneous effects of G, λ, π, and A on Y, p, r and $r_b \equiv r - \pi$. In other words, build a table similar to Table 2.1A in the text.

Hint: Use the following assumptions as you attempt to sign each expression:

$$D_r \equiv D_1\frac{\lambda}{1+\lambda}A + D_2 < 0,$$

$$D_\pi \equiv -D_1 A - D_2 > 0, \text{ and}$$

$$D_A \equiv D_3 + \left(r\frac{\lambda}{1+\lambda} - \pi\right)D_1 > 0.$$

Note that the assumption that $D_A > 0$ is a fairly stringent one, and yet a further restriction is necessary to sign the impact effect due to changes in A. What is this additional restriction? Also, make use of the recursive structure of the static equations to simplify things. In particular, note that p only enters one static equation.

Solution: The analogue to Table 2.1A for this economy is shown below.

	G	λ
Y	$-\dfrac{L_2}{J_2} > 0$	$\dfrac{A(D_r - rD_1 L_2)}{(1+\lambda)^2 J_2}$
p	$-\dfrac{\alpha L_2}{J_2} > 0$	$\dfrac{\alpha A(D_r - rD_1 L_2)}{(1+\lambda)^2 J_2}$
r	$\dfrac{L_1}{J_2} > 0$	$\dfrac{A((1-D_1) + rD_1 L_1)}{(1+\lambda)^2 J_2} > 0$
r_b	$\dfrac{L_1}{J_2} > 0$	$\dfrac{A((1-D_1) + rD_1 L_1)}{(1+\lambda)^2 J_2} > 0$

Note: The remaining two columns of this table are presented on the following page.

	π	A
Y	$-\dfrac{D_\pi L_2}{J_2} > 0$	$\dfrac{-L_2 D_A - \left(\dfrac{1}{1+\lambda} - L_3\right) D_r}{J_2}$
p	$-\dfrac{\alpha D_\pi L_2}{J_2} + 1 > 1$	$\dfrac{-\alpha L_2 D_A - \alpha\left(\dfrac{1}{1+\lambda} - L_3\right) D_r}{J_2}$
r	$\dfrac{D_\pi L_1}{J_2} > 0$	$\dfrac{L_1 D_A - \left(\dfrac{1}{1+\lambda} - L_3\right)(1 - D_1)}{J_2}$

$$r_b \qquad \frac{D_\pi L_1}{J_2} - 1 \qquad\qquad \frac{L_1 D_A - \left(\frac{1}{1+\lambda} - L_3\right)(1-D_1)}{J_2}$$

$$J_2 \equiv -L_2(1-D_1) - L_1 D_r > 0$$

Exercise 2.5

Assuming the pair of differential equations derived in Exercise 2.3 have a stable solution, linearize these equations about the steady state point and write the linearized system in matrix form.

Hint: Let $\dot{\pi} = g(\pi, A) = \gamma(p - \pi)$ *and* $\dot{A} = h(\pi, A) = G - T + r\dfrac{\lambda}{1+\lambda} A - pA$.

Now take a linear approximation to $g(\cdot)$ *and* $h(\cdot)$ *about the steady state point. Recall that Y, p, r, and* r_b *are instantaneous functions of G, T,* λ, π, *and A.*

Solution: The linearized system is given in matrix form below.

$$\begin{bmatrix}\dot{\pi}\\ \dot{A}\end{bmatrix} = \begin{bmatrix} \gamma\left(\dfrac{\partial p}{\partial \pi} - 1\right) & \gamma\dfrac{\partial p}{\partial A} \\ \left(\dfrac{\partial r}{\partial \pi}\dfrac{\lambda}{1+\lambda} - \dfrac{\partial p}{\partial \pi}\right)A & \left(r\dfrac{\lambda}{1+\lambda} - p\right) + \left(\dfrac{\partial r}{\partial A}\dfrac{\lambda}{1+\lambda} - \dfrac{\partial p}{\partial A}\right)A \end{bmatrix} \begin{bmatrix}\pi - \bar{\pi}\\ A - \bar{A}\end{bmatrix}$$

Each partial derivative in the above system represents an "impact effect" evaluated at the steady state point $(\pi, A) = (\bar{\pi}, \bar{A})$. If necessary, we could substitute the expressions for these partial derivatives, which we derived in Exercise 2.4, and attempt to simplify the resulting expressions.

Exercise 2.6

Derive the formal conditions for the system derived in Exercise 2.5 to have a stable solution.

Hint: See Exercise 2.2.

Solution: The following conditions must be satisfied if this system is to have a stable solution:

$$\gamma\left(\frac{\partial p}{\partial \pi}-1\right)+\left(r\frac{\lambda}{1+\lambda}-p\right)+\left(\frac{\partial r}{\partial A}\frac{\lambda}{1+\lambda}-\frac{\partial p}{\partial A}\right)A<0, \text{ and}$$

$$\left(\frac{\partial r}{\partial \pi}\frac{\lambda}{1+\lambda}-\frac{\partial p}{\partial \pi}\right)A\gamma\frac{\partial p}{\partial A}<0.$$

Once again, we could substitute in the derivative expressions found in Exercise 2.4 and attempt to simplify things.

Exercise 2.7

Write out the steady state equations for the system derived in Exercise 2.3. Of course, this presumes that the stability conditions of Exercise 2.6 are satisfied.

Hint: In steady state, when $\dot{\pi} = \dot{A} = 0$, we can see that:

$$\pi = p, \ Y = \overline{Y}, \text{ and } -T + r\frac{\lambda}{1+\lambda}A - pA = -G.$$

Solution: There are five steady state equations:

$$\overline{Y} - D(\overline{Y} - G, r - p, A) - G = 0,$$

$$A - (1+\lambda)L(\overline{Y}, r, A) = 0,$$

$$(G-T) + r\frac{\lambda}{1+\lambda}A - pA = 0,$$

$$Y - \overline{Y} = 0, \text{ and}$$

$$p - \pi = 0.$$

Exercise 2.8

Assume the economic system described in the past several exercises is initially in steady state. Determine the long run effect of changes in G and λ upon r, p and A, which are endogenously determined by the first three steady state equations derived in Exercise 2.7. Try to sign the expressions. In order to keep the algebra more manageable, assume (purely for convenience) that

$$L_3 = \frac{1}{1+\lambda}.$$

Chapter 2

Hint: Totally differentiate the first three steady state equations, holding $\overline{Y}$ and T fixed in all cases, and varying one exogenous parameter at a time. When you attempt to sign expressions, make the added assumption that

$$r\frac{\lambda}{1+\lambda} - p > 0.$$

Solution: The requested comparative static expressions are shown below, in a format which is similar to Table 2.1B in the text.

	G	λ
r	0	$\dfrac{-A}{(1+\lambda)J_0}[AD_3 - D_2\Omega] > 0$
p	$\dfrac{(1+\lambda)L_2}{J_0}[D_3 - (1-D_1)\Omega]$	$\dfrac{1}{J_0}\left[\dfrac{D_2 A}{1+\lambda}\Omega + D_3\left[\dfrac{rAL_2}{1+\lambda} - \dfrac{A^2\lambda}{(1+\lambda)^2}\right]\right] > 0$
A	$\dfrac{(1+\lambda)L_2}{J_0}[D_2 + A(1-D_1)]$	$\dfrac{D_2}{J_0}\left[\dfrac{A^2}{(1+\lambda)^2} + \dfrac{rAL_2}{(1+\lambda)}\right]$

$$\Omega \equiv r\frac{\lambda}{1+\lambda} - p \ ; \ J_0 \equiv (1+\lambda)L_2\left[-D_2\left(r\frac{\lambda}{1+\lambda} - p\right) + AD_3\right] < 0 \quad \text{if} \quad \Omega > 0$$

3 Rational Expectations: Some Basic Issues

Exercise 3.1

Suppose the central bank announces at time zero that it will double the money stock at time $T > 0$. That is,

$m(t) = \overline{m}$ for $0 \leq t \leq T$, and

$m(t) = 2\overline{m}$ for $t \geq T$.

Describe the time path of the price level following this announcement, using equation (3.21) in the text. Derive an expression for the size of the "announcement jump" in $p(t)$ at time $t = 0$.

Hint: Consider the solutions for $0 \leq t \leq T$ and $t \geq T$ separately. For the former, split the integral in (3.21) into two integrals.

Solution: Prior to the announcement, we have $p*(0) = \overline{m}$. After the announcement, we have

$$p(t) = \overline{m}\left[e^{(t-T)/\alpha} + 1\right],$$

so the announcement jump is:

$$p(0) - p*(0) = \overline{m} e^{-T/\alpha} > 0.$$

Note that the magnitude of the upward jump is a decreasing function of the amount of lead time, T, between announcement and implementation of the policy change.

Exercise 3.2

Suppose the money stock is constant through time T and them begins growing at rate $\mu < 1/\alpha$ from then on. Agents know at time zero that this change will occur. The money supply process is therefore given by:

$m(t) = \overline{m}$ for $0 \le t \le T$, and

$m(t) = \overline{m} e^{\mu t}$ for $t \ge T$.

Use equation (3.21) in the text to solve for the time path of the price level in this situation.

Hint: None.

Solution: the time path of the price level is described by the following equations:

$$p(t) = \overline{m}\left\{1-\left[1+\frac{e^{\mu T}}{\alpha\mu-1}\right]e^{(t-T)/\alpha}\right\} \quad for \quad 0 \le t \le T, \text{ and}$$

$$p(t) = \frac{\overline{m} e^{\mu t}}{1-\alpha\mu} \quad for \quad t \ge T.$$

Whether the jump at time T is up or down depends on α and μ.

Exercise 3.3

What is the immediate effect on the price level at the time the monetary policy change described in Exercise 3.2 is announced? What effect does the amount of lead time between announcement and implementation have on the immediate price adjustment?

Hint: Compare p(0) before and after the announcement, using the assumption that $\mu < 1/\alpha$.

Solution: The price level jumps up (down) at time zero if $e^{\mu T} > (<) \ 1-\alpha\mu$. A longer lead time (greater T) makes an upward jump more likely.

Exercise 3.4

Consider the Cagan model equation:

$$m_t - p_t = -\gamma(E_t p_{t+1} - p_t) \ , \quad \gamma > 0,$$

where $m_t \equiv ln(M_t)$ and $p_t \equiv ln(P_t)$. Suppose agents know that the natural logarithm of the money supply follows the random walk:

$$m_{t+1} = m_t + \varepsilon_{t+1},$$

where ε_{t+1} is a white noise error term. Find the rational expectations equilibrium value of p_t by the method of undetermined coefficients.

Hint: Since m_t follows a random walk, all information regarding past realizations of the log of the money stock are contained in its present value. Use this fact to simplify your initial guess on the form of the solution.

Solution: $p_t = m_t$.

Exercise 3.5

Does the model outlined in Exercise 3.4 possess an unstable "bubble" solution? If so, what form does it take?

Hint: The method of iterated expectations may be more revealing here.

Solution: Yes, there are an infinite number of bubble solution of the form:

$$p_t = m_t + A_t,$$

where the stochastic process $\{A_t\}$ satisfies the stochastic difference equation

$$E_t A_{t+1} = \frac{1+\gamma}{\gamma} A_t$$

for all t.

Exercise 3.6

Assume the price level is determined by the same model used in Exercises 3.4 and 3.5:

$$m_t - p_t = -\gamma(E_t p_{t+1} - p_t) \quad , \quad \gamma > 0.$$

Suppose the monetary authority pursues a policy of gradually adjusting the money supply back toward a fixed level, $\overline{m}$, according to the following process:

$$m_{t+1} = \alpha(m_t - \overline{m}) + \varepsilon_{t+1} \quad , \quad -1 < \alpha < 0.$$

Agents know about this policy, including the parameter α. Derive the rational expectations equilibrium expression for p_t, using the method of undetermined coefficients.

Hint: Since the money stock follows a first order process, a simplified guess at the form of the solution for p_t should be apparent.

Solution: $p_t = \dfrac{m_t - \alpha\gamma\overline{m}}{1 + \gamma - \alpha\gamma}$.

It is a good idea to check whether the solution to a linear rational expectations model actually satisfies the original model and/or the expectational difference equation you started from. In this case, it is not at all difficult to do so.

Exercise 3.7

Consider the following slight modification of equations (3.44a) and (3.44b) in the text.

$$y_t = a + b y^*_{t,t-1} + c x_t$$

$$x_t = \rho_1 x_{t-1} + \rho_2 x_{t-2} + v_t$$

The agent knows ρ_1 and ρ_2, but not a, b and c. He gradually learns the true coefficients in the reduced form equilibrium expression for y_t. Derive the updating equations, by which the agent's perceptions of these coefficients are updated.

Hint: First derive the rational expectations solution to the model, replacing y_{t-1}^* with $E_{t-1} y_t$. Follow the steps described at the start of Section 3.7 in the text.

Solution: The updating equations are:

$$\alpha_{n+1} = a + b\alpha_n, \quad \beta_{n+1} = b\beta_n + c\rho_1, \quad \delta_{n+1} = b\delta_n + c\rho_2, \text{ and } \gamma_{n+1} = c.$$

Note that the agent's perceptions will converge to the true rational expectations coefficients eventually, so long as $|b| < 1$.

4 Rational Expectations and Policy Neutrality

Exercise 4.1

Suppose random variables X and Y are jointly normally distributed as follows:

$$\begin{bmatrix} X \\ Y \end{bmatrix} \sim N\left(\begin{bmatrix} \mu_X \\ \mu_Y \end{bmatrix}, \begin{bmatrix} \sigma_{XX} & \sigma_{XY} \\ \sigma_{XY} & \sigma_{YY} \end{bmatrix} \right).$$

Write down the expression for $E(X \mid X+Y)$.

Hint: Write down the expression for the fitted value from a bivariate regression of X on $X+Y$, using population moments rather than sample moments.

Solution:

$$E(X \mid X+Y) = \mu_X + \frac{\sigma_{XX} + \sigma_{XY}}{\sigma_{XX} + 2\sigma_{XY} + \sigma_{YY}} \left[(X+Y) - (\mu_X + \mu_Y) \right].$$

Exercise 4.2

Consider the following simple macroeconomic model.

$$y_t = \gamma(p_t - E_{t-1} p_t) + \lambda y_{t-1}$$

$$m_t - p_t = y_t$$

$$m_t = \alpha - \beta y_{t-1} + u_t - \rho u_{t-1}$$

All parameters are strictly positive and known to everyone. The parameter β represents a feedback policy on the part of the monetary authority, presumably intended to help stabilize output. Solve for y_t in terms of exogenous and predetermined variables. Is the feedback policy effective in this economy?

Hint: Use the method of undetermined coefficients. It may help to manipulate the equations, yielding an equation in y_t, $E_{t-1}y_t$ and u_t, (but not p_t or m_t), prior to guessing the form of the solution for y_t.

Solution: $y_t = \lambda y_{t-1} + \dfrac{\gamma}{1+\gamma} u_t$.

The fact that β does not appear implies that the monetary feedback rule is ineffective.

Exercise 4.3

Solve the following macroeconomic model for y_t, assuming that expectations are formed rationally.

$$y_t = \gamma(p_t - E_{t-1}p_t) + u_t \quad , \quad \gamma > 0$$

$$m_t - p_t = y_t$$

$$m_t = \delta m_{t-1} + \varepsilon_t \quad , \quad 0 < \delta < 1$$

Use the resulting expression for y_t and the following arbitrage condition to determine the (log) equilibrium price of equities, q_t.

$$r = \theta(E_t q_{t+1} - q_t) + (1-\theta)(y_t - q_t) \quad , \quad 0 < \theta < 1$$

The variable r is the real interest rate, which is assumed to be constant.

Hint: The hint for Exercise 4.2 applies here as well.

Solution:

$$y_t = \dfrac{1}{1+\gamma} u_t + \dfrac{\gamma}{1+\gamma} \varepsilon_t$$

$$q_t = \dfrac{r}{\theta - 1} + (1-\theta)\left[\dfrac{1}{1+\gamma} u_t + \dfrac{\gamma}{1+\gamma} \varepsilon_t\right]$$

Exercise 4.4

Suppose prices are partly predetermined and partly determined by market forces:

$$p_t = E_{t-1} p_t + \gamma(m_t - p_t) \quad , \quad \gamma > 0.$$

Aggregate demand is given by

$$y_t = m_t - p_t,$$

and the money supply process is given by

$$m_t = \delta m_{t-1} + \varepsilon_t \quad , \text{where} \quad 0 < \delta < 1.$$

Solve for p_t and y_t.

Hint: It is possible to solve this model without resorting to either the method of iterated expectations or the method of undetermined coefficients. The short-cut method begins by applying the $E_{t-1}(\cdot)$ operator to the first equation.

Solution:

$$p_t = \delta m_{t-1} + \frac{\gamma}{1+\gamma} \varepsilon_t$$

$$y_t = \frac{1}{1+\gamma} \varepsilon_t$$

Exercise 4.5

Suppose the log of output is determined by

$$y_t = \delta\left(w_t - E_{t-1} w_t\right),$$

where w_t is the log of the wage at time t. The log of labor demand and labor supply are given respectively by

$$L_t^d = -\alpha\left(w_t - p_t\right), \text{ and}$$

$$L_t^s = \beta(w_t - p_t),$$

where p_t is the log of the price level, and the parameters α and β are positive numbers. Assuming the labor market always clears, derive a Lucas supply function from the equations given above.

Hint: None.

Solution: $y_t = \delta(p_t - E_{t-1} p_t)$

Exercise 4.6

Suppose the log of the money supply follows a random walk:

$$m_t = m_{t-1} + \varepsilon_t.$$

Let aggregate demand be given by

$$y_t = m_t - p_t.$$

Now, using the Lucas supply curve you derived in Exercise 4.5, determine the rational expectations solution for y_t.

Hint: Manipulate the equations to eliminate p_t and m_t, leaving a stochastic difference equation involving y_t. Apply the method of undetermined coefficients to solve it.

Solution: $y_t = \dfrac{\delta}{1+\delta} \varepsilon_t.$

Exercise 4.7

This question is adapted from Problem #6 at the end of Chapter 15 of Thomas Sargent's *Macroeconomic Theory* (1979, Academic Press). Consider the following macroeconomic model:

$$y_t = \gamma(p_t - E_{t-1} p_t) + \lambda y_{t-1} + \varepsilon_t, \quad \gamma > 0, 0 < \lambda < 1$$

$$m_t - p_t = (1-\tau)y_t + u_t, \quad 0 < \tau < 1$$

$$m_t = \alpha + \beta_1 \varepsilon_{t-1} + \beta_2 \varepsilon_{t-2} + \delta_1 u_{t-1} + \delta_2 u_{t-2}$$

Assume ε_t and u_t are independent white noise errors, while τ represents the marginal income tax rate. The monetary authority pursues a second order feedback rule, presumably to try to minimize some quadratic loss function of p_t and y_t. Solve for p_t and y_t, assuming rational expectations. Does the feedback rule affect real output in equilibrium?

Hint: This is similar to the past few exercises, but the algebra is a little messier this time.

Solution: The reduced form solutions for p_t and y_t are given below.

$$p_t = \alpha - \frac{(1-\tau)\varepsilon_t}{1+\gamma(1-\tau)} + \beta_1 \varepsilon_{t-1} + \beta_2 \varepsilon_{t-2} - \frac{u_t}{1+\gamma(1-\tau)} + \delta_1 u_{t-1}$$
$$+ \delta_2 u_{t-2} - \lambda(1-\tau) y_{t-1}$$

$$y_t = \frac{\varepsilon_t - \gamma u_t}{1+\gamma(1-\tau)} + \lambda y_{t-1}$$

The feedback rule has no effect on real output.

5 Nonuniqueness Issues in Rational Expectations Models

Exercise 5.1

The following model is very similar to the one presented in Section 5.1 of the text. The most significant difference is that the money supply is not constant over time in this model.

$$y = -d_1\left[r_t - \left(p^*_{t+1,t-1} - p^*_{t,t-1}\right)\right] + u_{1t}$$

$$m_t - p_t = y_t - \alpha_1 r_t + \alpha_2(m_t - p_t) + u_{2t}$$

$$y_t = \gamma_1(m_t - p_t) + u_{3t}$$

$$m_t = \overline{m} + \varepsilon_t + \theta\varepsilon_{t-1}$$

Reduce this system to an expectational difference equation in p_t, which is driven by monetary shocks and a composite shock, $u_t = f(u_{1t}, u_{2t}, u_{3t})$. Solve for all of the rational expectations equilibrium solutions to this difference equation.

Hint: The solutions may contain a constant and could depend on all current and past values of u_t and ε_t. There will be an infinite number of solutions, because you will not be able to determine specific values for two of the reduced form coefficients.

Solution: The expectational difference equation for the price level is

$$E_{t-1}p_{t+1} = E_{t-1}p_t + \delta_1 p_t + u_t - \delta_1\overline{m} - \delta_1\varepsilon_t - \delta_1\theta\varepsilon_{t-1}, \text{ where}$$

$$\delta_1 = -\frac{1-\alpha_2}{\alpha_1} - \gamma_1\left(\frac{1}{\alpha_1} + \frac{1}{d_1}\right), \text{ and}$$

$$u_t = -\frac{1}{d_1}u_{1t} + \frac{1}{\alpha_1}u_{2t} + \left(\frac{1}{\alpha_1} + \frac{1}{d_1}\right)u_{3t}.$$

We postulate a general form for the solution:

$$p_t = \bar{p} + \sum_{i=0}^{\infty}\pi_i u_{t-i} + \sum_{i=0}^{\infty}\lambda_i \varepsilon_{t-i},$$

where $\bar{p}$, π_i and λ_i $(i = 0,1,2,...)$ are all undetermined coefficients. After applying the usual methods, π_1 and λ_1 are still undetermined, though we are able to solve for the other coefficients:

$$\bar{p} = \bar{m} \quad , \quad \pi_0 = -\frac{1}{\delta_1} \quad , \quad \lambda_0 = 1 \quad ,$$

$$\pi_i = (1+\delta_1)^{i-1}\pi_1 \quad for \quad i = 1, 2,...$$

$$\lambda_i = (1+\delta_1)^{i-1}\lambda_1 - (1+\delta_1)^{i-2}\delta_1\theta \quad for \quad i = 2, 3,...$$

Plugging these expressions into the original guess yields the following set of solutions:

$$p_t = \bar{m} - \frac{1}{\delta_1}u_t + \pi_1\sum_{i=0}^{\infty}(1+\delta_1)^i u_{t-i-1} + \varepsilon_t + \lambda_1\varepsilon_{t-1} + \left(\lambda_1 - \frac{\delta_1\theta}{1+\delta_1}\right)\sum_{i=1}^{\infty}(1+\delta_1)^i\varepsilon_{t-i-1}$$

By varying π_1 and λ_1, we arrive at an infinite number of solutions, which are all stable, so long as the restriction $-2 < \delta_1 < 0$ holds.

Exercise 5.2

Calculate the unconditional variance of p_t, using the general solution derived in Exercise 5.1. Assume that $-2 < \delta_1 < 0$, so each of the solutions has a finite variance. Derive expressions for π_1 and λ_1 that satisfy the criterion suggested by Taylor for choosing among stable rational expectations solutions, and substitute these expressions into the general solution you found in Exercise 5.1, resulting in a unique minimum variance solution.

Hint: Recall that $var(aX + bY) = a^2 var(X) + b^2 var(Y)$, if X and Y are uncorrelated and a and b are constants.

Solution: The unconditional variance of p_t $(var(p_t) \equiv \sigma_p^2)$ is

$$\sigma_p^2 = \left[\left(\frac{1}{\delta_1}\right)^2 + \pi_1^2 \sum_{i=0}^{\infty}(1+\delta_1)^{2i}\right]\sigma_u^2 + \left[1+\lambda_1^2 + \left(\lambda_1 - \frac{\delta_1\theta}{1+\delta_1}\right)^2 \sum_{i=1}^{\infty}(1+\delta_1)^{2i}\right]\sigma_\varepsilon^2$$

the expressions for π_1 and λ_1 that minimize σ_p^2 are: $\pi_1 = 0$ and $\lambda_1 = \delta_1(1+\delta_1)\theta$. Substitute these expressions into the general solution derived in Exercise 5.1, resulting in the following unique minimum variance solution.

$$p_t = \overline{m} - \frac{u_t}{\delta_1} + \varepsilon_t + \delta_1(1+\delta_1)\theta\varepsilon_{t-1} + \delta_1(1+\delta_1)\theta\left(1 - \frac{1}{(1+\delta_1)^2}\right)\sum_{i=1}^{\infty}(1+\delta_1)^i \varepsilon_{t-i-1}$$

Exercise 5.3

The model given below is identical to the one given in Exercise 5.1, except that the expected rate of inflation is now defined to be conditional on a time t information set, and the monetary policy rule responds contemporaneously to the price level.

$$y_t = -d_1\left[r_t - \left(p_{t+1,t}^* - p_t\right)\right] + u_{1t}$$

$$m_t - p_t = y_t - \alpha_1 r_t + \alpha_2(m_t - p_t) + u_{2t}$$

$$y_t = \gamma_1(m_t - p_t) + u_{3t}$$

$$m_t = \overline{m} - \beta p_t + \varepsilon_t$$

As in Exercise 5.1, we assume that the errors are not correlated with one another. Solve this model for an expectational difference equation in p_t, which is driven by ε_t and $u_t = f(u_{1t}, u_{2t}, u_{3t})$. Derive an equation for p_t which, by varying the remaining unidentified coefficients, defines all of the rational expectations solutions to the expectational difference equation.

Hint: Some of the work you did for Exercise 5.1 should be helpful here.

Solution: The expectational difference equation for the price level is

$$E_t p_{t+1} = -\delta_1 \overline{m} + (1+\delta_1 + \beta\delta_1)p_t + u_t - \delta_1 \varepsilon_t, \text{ where}$$

$$\delta_1 = -\frac{1-\alpha_2}{\alpha_1} - \gamma_1\left(\frac{1}{\alpha_1} + \frac{1}{d_1}\right), \text{ and}$$

$$u_t = -\frac{1}{d_1}u_{1t} + \frac{1}{\alpha_1}u_{2t} + \left(\frac{1}{\alpha_1} + \frac{1}{d_1}\right)u_{3t}.$$

We postulate a solution of the following general form:

$$p_t = \bar{p} + \sum_{i=0}^{\infty}\pi_i u_{t-i} + \sum_{i=0}^{\infty}\lambda_i \varepsilon_{t-i}$$

where $\bar{p}$, π_i and λ_i $(i = 0,1,2,...)$ are all undetermined coefficients. In this case, we are unable to identify π_0 and λ_0 in terms of the underlying model parameters. However, we are able to determine the rest of the coefficients:

$$\bar{p} = \frac{m}{1+\beta},$$

$$\pi_i = \pi_0(1+\delta_1+\beta\delta_1)^i + (1+\delta_1+\beta\delta_1)^{i-1} \quad \text{for} \quad i = 1, 2,...$$

$$\lambda_i = \lambda_0(1+\delta_1+\beta\delta_1)^i - \delta_1(1+\delta_1+\beta\delta_1)^{i-1} \quad \text{for} \quad i = 1, 2,...$$

Substitute these expressions into the postulated general form of the solution.

$$p_t = \frac{m}{1+\beta} + \pi_0 u_t + \lambda_0 \varepsilon_t + \left[\pi_0(1+\delta_1+\beta\delta_1)+1\right]\sum_{i=0}^{\infty}(1+\delta_1+\beta\delta_1)^i u_{t-i-1}$$
$$+ \left[\lambda_0(1+\delta_1+\beta\delta_1)-\delta_1\right]\sum_{i=0}^{\infty}(1+\delta_1+\beta\delta_1)^i \varepsilon_{t-i-1}$$

By varying π_1 and λ_1, we arrive at an infinite number of solutions for p_t. Assuming that $|1+\delta_1+\beta\delta_1| < 1$, all of these solutions are stable.

Exercise 5.4

Calculate the unconditional variance of p_t, using the general solution derived in Exercise 5.3. Assume that the stability condition, $|1+\delta_1+\beta\delta_1| < 1$, does hold. Derive expressions for π_0 and λ_0 that satisfy the criterion suggested by Taylor for choosing among stable rational expectations solutions. Substitute these expressions into the general solution derived in Exercise 5.3, resulting in a unique minimum variance solution.

Hint: It may be helpful to make a change of index variables in one or more places, using an identity like: $\sum_{i=1}^{\infty} \phi^{i-1} x_{t-i} \equiv \sum_{i=0}^{\infty} \phi^{i} x_{t-(i+1)} \equiv \sum_{i=0}^{\infty} \phi^{i} x_{t-i-1}$, $|\phi| < 1$.

Solution: The unconditional variance of p_t $(var(p_t) \equiv \sigma_p^2)$ is:

$$\sigma_p^2 = \left\{ \pi_0^2 + \frac{\left[\pi_0(1+\delta_1+\beta\delta_1)+1\right]^2}{1-(1+\delta_1+\beta\delta_1)^2} \right\} \sigma_u^2 + \left\{ \lambda_0^2 + \frac{\left[\lambda_0(1+\delta_1+\beta\delta_1)-\delta_1\right]^2}{1-(1+\delta_1+\beta\delta_1)^2} \right\} \sigma_\varepsilon^2.$$

The expressions for π_0 and λ_0 that minimize σ_p^2 are: $\pi_0 = -(1+\delta_1+\beta\delta_1)$ and $\lambda_0 = \delta_1(1+\delta_1+\beta\delta_1)$. Substitute these expressions into the general solution derived in Exercise 5.3, resulting in the following unique minimum variance solution:

$$p_t = \frac{\overline{m}}{1+\beta} - (1+\delta_1+\beta\delta_1)(u_t - \delta_1\varepsilon_t)$$
$$+ \left[1-(1+\delta_1+\beta\delta_1)^2\right]\sum_{i=0}^{\infty}(1+\delta_1+\beta\delta_1)^i (u_{t-i-1} - \delta_1\varepsilon_{t-i-1})$$

Exercise 5.5

Solve the following rational expectations model for the price level, p_t.

$$y = \alpha\left[r - (E_t p_{t+1} - p_t)\right] + u_t \quad , \quad \alpha < 0$$
$$m_t - p_t = \beta y_t + \varepsilon_t \quad , \quad \beta > 0$$
$$m_t = -\lambda p_{t-1} + \varepsilon_t \quad , \quad \lambda <> 0$$

If there are multiple equlibria, choose the expression(s) for p_t whose reduced form coefficients vary continuously with the policy parameter, λ. Determine any restrictions on λ that are necessary to ensure real solutions for p_t.

Hint: Utilize the minimum state variable criterion when applying the method of undetermined coefficients.

Solution: By combining the three model equations, we arrive at the following stochastic difference equation for the price level:

$$E_t p_{t+1} = r + \frac{1+\alpha\beta}{\alpha} p_t + \frac{\lambda}{\alpha\beta} p_{t-1} + \frac{1}{\alpha\beta}\varepsilon_t + \frac{1}{\alpha} u_t$$

The simplest solution to this difference equation has p_t depending on a constant, ε_t, u_t and p_{t-1}. Thus, in accordance with the minimum state variable criterion, we postulate that

$$p_t = \bar{p} + \pi_0 \varepsilon_t + \pi_1 u_t + \pi_2 p_{t-1},$$

where $\bar{p}$, π_0, π_1 and π_2 are coefficients to be determined. We find that:

$$\bar{p} = \frac{\alpha\beta r}{\alpha\beta\pi_2 - 1},$$

$$\pi_0 = \frac{1}{\alpha\beta\pi_2 - \alpha\beta - 1},$$

$$\pi_1 = \frac{\beta}{\alpha\beta\pi_2 - \alpha\beta - 1}, \text{ and}$$

$$\pi_2 = \frac{1}{2}\frac{1+\alpha\beta}{\alpha\beta} \pm \frac{1}{2}\sqrt{\left(\frac{1+\alpha\beta}{\alpha\beta}\right)^2 + \frac{4\lambda}{\alpha\beta}}.$$

π_2 is continuous as λ varies about zero only if we choose the root

$$\pi_2 = \frac{1}{2}\frac{1+\alpha\beta}{\alpha\beta} - \frac{1}{2}\sqrt{\left(\frac{1+\alpha\beta}{\alpha\beta}\right)^2 + \frac{4\lambda}{\alpha\beta}}.$$

Substitute the expressions for $\bar{p}$, π_0, π_1 and π_2 into the original postulated solution to derive the reduced form expression for p_t. The equilibrium price level in this model is a real number so long as

$$\lambda \geq -\frac{1}{4}\frac{(1+\alpha\beta)^2}{\alpha\beta}.$$

Exercise 5.6

This exercise and the next one are based upon a model developed by Bennett McCallum, as presented by William Scarth in *Macroeconomics: An Intro-*

duction to Advanced Methods (1988, Harcourt Brace Jovanovich). Firm i chooses a price for its output, p_t^i, so as to minimize the output adjustment cost function,

$$c_t = \delta_1 \left[E_{t-1}(y_t^i) \right]^2 + \delta_2 \left[E_{t-1}(y_t^i) - y_{t-1}^i \right]^2 \quad , \quad \delta_1, \delta_2 > 0,$$

subject to its perceived demand function,

$$E_{t-1}(y_t^i) = -\eta \left[p_t^i - E_{t-1}(p_t^*) \right] \quad , \quad \eta > 0,$$

where p_t^* represents the "going market price." Output and prices are expressed in logarithmic terms, and we choose units such that the natural level of output is $\bar{y}_t = 0$. Output variations from this natural level and changes in output that vary from changes in $\bar{y}_t$ are costly, as reflected in the expression for c_t. The firm loses (gains) sales if it sets its price above (below) the going market price. Derive a pricing rule for firm i that satisfies its constrained minimization problem.

Hint: At time t, there is no uncertainty about the level of output in the previous period, so $y_{t-1}^i = -\eta \left[p_{t-1}^i - p_{t-1}^* \right]$.

Solution: The price-setting rule is to choose p_t^i such that

$$p_t^i - E_{t-1} p_t^* = (1-\phi)\left(p_{t-1}^i - p_{t-1}^* \right).$$

Exercise 5.7

Assume all firms are identical and follow the price-setting rule derived in Exercise 5.6:

$$p_t - E_{t-1} p_t^* = (1-\phi)\left(p_{t-1} - p_{t-1}^* \right).$$

Suppose aggregate demand is given by

$$y_t = -\theta p_t + v_t,$$

where v_t is a white noise error term. Derive rational expectations solutions for y_t and p_t under two different assumptions regarding the determination of the "going market price" p_t^*.

Case 1: p_t^* is set so that output equals its natural level, $\bar{y}_t = 0$.

Case 2: $p_t^* = 0$, which is assumed to be its long run average value.

Compute the unconditional variances σ_y^2 and σ_p^2 for each case. Which case is consistent with Taylor's minimum variance criterion for choosing among multiple rational expectations equilibria? Is this an economically sensible choice?

Hint: You can easily solve the model in both cases, without resorting to either the method of undetermined coefficients or the method of iterated expectations.

Solution:

Case 1:

$$y_t = (1-\phi)y_{t-1} + v_t \quad ; \quad \sigma_y^2 = \frac{1}{1-(1-\phi)^2}\sigma_v^2$$

$$p_t = \left[\frac{-(1-\phi)}{\theta}\right]y_{t-1} \quad ; \quad \sigma_p^2 = \left[\frac{1-\phi}{\theta}\right]^2 \sigma_y^2$$

Case 2:

$$y_t = (1-\phi)y_{t-1} + v_t - (1-\phi)v_{t-1} \quad ; \quad \sigma_y^2 = \sigma_v^2$$

$$p_t = \left[\frac{(1-\phi)}{\theta}\right](v_{t-1} - y_{t-1}) \quad ; \quad \sigma_p^2 = \left[\frac{1-\phi}{\theta}\right]^2 (\sigma_y^2 - \sigma_v^2) = 0$$

According to Taylor's criterion, we should accept the Case 2 solutions. Others might argue for excluding this case as "nonfundamental," since the assumption by firms that $p_t^* = 0$ must come from outside the model.

6 Rational Expectations and Saddlepoint Behavior

Exercise 6.1

The following model, which is due to Olivier Blanchard (1981, *American Economic Review*, 71,132-43), is presented by William Scarth in his book entitled *Macroeconomics: An Introduction to Advanced Methods* (1988, Harcourt Brace Jovanovich).

$$\dot{Y} = \sigma(aq + bY + g - Y) \qquad a > 0, 0 < b < 1, \sigma > 0$$

$$r = cY - \ell M \qquad c > 0, \ell > 0$$

$$r = \frac{jY + \dot{q}}{q} \qquad j > 0$$

The variables are defined as follows:

$Y \equiv$ output

$q \equiv$ price of equities

$r \equiv$ rate of return on equities

$G \equiv$ government expenditures

$M \equiv$ money supply

You can interpret the equations given above as a version of the IS / LM model with sluggish output adjustment. While the flow of output is restricted to change continuously over time, we assume that the price of equities is a jump variable.

Derive a two equation dynamic system from the given model, which governs the evolution of q and Y over time. Assume the system is stable for now and write down the steady state equations. Determine the comparative static effects of a permanent change in G and of a permanent change in M.

Hint: Assume $r = cY - \ell M > 0$ in all of the analysis related to this model.

Solution: The two dynamic system is given by the following differential pair of equations:

$$\dot{q}(t) = [cq(t) - j]Y(t) - q(t)\ell M(t)$$
$$\dot{Y}(t) = \sigma[aq(t) + bY(t) + G(t) - Y(t)]$$

The exogenous policy parameters, $G(t)$ and $M(t)$, might vary over time in some general fashion, but we will only consider once-and-for-all changes in these variables. The steady state equations may be written in the following way:

$$q = \frac{jY}{cY - \ell M} \qquad (\dot{q} = 0 \text{ locus})$$

$$q = \frac{1-b}{a}Y - \frac{1}{a}G \qquad (\dot{Y} = 0 \text{ locus})$$

The comparative static effects of changes in G and M on q and Y are shown below, where an over-bar above a variable denotes the steady state (i.e., long run) value of the variable.

$$\frac{\partial \bar{q}}{\partial G} = \frac{1}{\Delta} \frac{-j\ell M}{a(cY - \ell M)^2} < 0 \qquad \frac{\partial \bar{Y}}{\partial G} = \frac{1}{\Delta}\frac{1}{a} > 0$$

$$\frac{\partial \bar{q}}{\partial M} = \frac{1}{\Delta} \frac{(1-b)j\ell Y}{a(cY - \ell M)^2} > 0 \qquad \frac{\partial \bar{Y}}{\partial M} = \frac{1}{\Delta}\frac{j\ell Y}{(cY - \ell M)^2} > 0$$

$$\Delta \equiv \frac{j\ell M}{(cY - \ell M)^2} + \frac{1-b}{a} > 0$$

Recall that we have assumed that $cY - \ell M = r > 0$.

Exercise 6.2

Linearize the dynamic system from Exercise 6.1 about the steady state point $(\bar{Y}, \bar{q})$, and note a sufficient condition to ensure that the linearized system will be stable. Use a phase diagram to characterize the complete dynamic adjustment following a once-and-for-all increase in government expenditures, which is implemented at the same time that it is announced. Perform a similar analysis for a permanent increase in the money supply.

Hint: Sketch the steady state loci, which divide the first quadrant of Y,q-space into four regions. Determine the direction of motion for Y and q in each of these regions.

Solution: The linearized system is

$$\begin{bmatrix} \dot{q}(t) \\ \dot{Y}(t) \end{bmatrix} = \begin{bmatrix} \bar{r} & c\bar{q} - j \\ \sigma a & -\sigma(1-b) \end{bmatrix} \begin{bmatrix} q(t) - \bar{q} \\ Y(t) - \bar{Y} \end{bmatrix},$$

where $\bar{r} = c\bar{Y} - \ell M$ is the steady state rate of interest. Stability requires that

$$-\sigma(1-b)\bar{r} - \sigma a(c\bar{q} - j) < 0,$$

which will certainly hold if $\bar{r} > 0$ and $c\bar{q} - j > 0$.

Recall the equations from Exercise 6.1, which describe the steady state loci:

$$q = \frac{jY}{cY - \ell M} \qquad (\dot{q} = 0 \ locus)$$

$$q = \frac{1-b}{a}Y - \frac{1}{a}G \qquad (\dot{Y} = 0 \ locus)$$

Note that the $\dot{q} = 0$ locus is downward-sloping in Y,q-space, while the $\dot{Y} = 0$ locus slopes upward. Also, if we place q on the vertical axis and Y on the horizontal axis, we see that an increase in G shifts the $\dot{Y} = 0$ locus down and to the right, while an increase in M shifts the $\dot{q} = 0$ locus up and to the right.

A phase diagram depicting the effects of a permanent (and immediate) increase in G is shown below. There is an immediate jump from point 1 to point 2, followed by an adjustment over time along the new stable arm, S'S', to the new steady state at point 3.

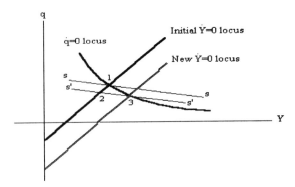

The following phase diagram depicts the dynamic response to a permanent (and immediate) increase in M. Notice that there is overshooting in the price of equities, as we jump immediately to point 2, before converging along S'S' to the new steady state point 3.

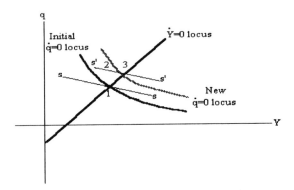

Exercise 6.3

Suppose the economy described by the pair of linear differential equations you derived in Exercise 6.2 is in the long run equilibrium at time t=0, when it is announced that a permanent increase in the money supply will be implemented at time $T > 0$. Derive a set of four equations that describe the evolution of $q(t)$ and $Y(t)$ during the time frames $0 < t \leq T$ and $t \geq T$. Show that the initial jump in $q(t)$ at the time of the announcement is a decreasing function of the amount of implementation lead time, T. In order to simplify this analysis, ignore the fact that the characteristic roots of the system actually depend on M.

Hint: Solve for the constants of integration in terms of $d\bar{q} \equiv \bar{q}_2 - \bar{q}_1$ and $d\bar{Y} \equiv \bar{Y}_2 - \bar{Y}_1$, where $(\bar{Y}_1, \bar{q}_1)$ is the original steady state, and $(\bar{Y}_2, \bar{q}_2)$ is the new steady state. In this case,

$$d\bar{Y} = \frac{\partial \bar{Y}}{\partial M} dM \quad \text{and} \quad d\bar{q} = \frac{\partial \bar{q}}{\partial M} dM,$$

but that only affects the interpretation of the solution.

Solution: The following equations describe the evolution of $q(t)$ and $Y(t)$ during the two time frames of interest.

$0 < t \leq T$:

$$q(t) = \bar{q}_1 + \frac{d\bar{q} - \phi_1 d\bar{Y}}{e^{\lambda_2 T}(\lambda_1 - \lambda_2)}\left[(\lambda_1 + \sigma(1-b))e^{\lambda_1 t} - (\lambda_2 + \sigma(1-b))e^{\lambda_2 t}\right]$$

$$Y(t) = \bar{Y}_1 + \sigma a \frac{d\bar{q} - \phi_1 d\bar{Y}}{e^{\lambda_2 T}(\lambda_1 - \lambda_2)}\left[e^{\lambda_1 t} - e^{\lambda_2 t}\right]$$

$t \geq T$:

$$q(t) = \bar{q}_2 + \frac{(\lambda_1 + \sigma(1-b))}{\lambda_1 - \lambda_2}\left[\frac{d\bar{q} - \phi_1 d\bar{Y}}{e^{\lambda_2 T}} - \frac{d\bar{q} - \phi_2 d\bar{Y}}{e^{\lambda_1 T}}\right]e^{\lambda_1 t}$$

$$Y(t) = \bar{Y}_2 + \frac{\sigma a}{\lambda_1 - \lambda_2}\left[\frac{d\bar{q} - \phi_1 d\bar{Y}}{e^{\lambda_2 T}} - \frac{d\bar{q} - \phi_2 d\bar{Y}}{e^{\lambda_1 T}}\right]e^{\lambda_1 t}$$

We define λ_1 as the stable (negative) root of the linearized dynamic system, with corresponding eigenvector $[\phi_1 \ 1]'$ and λ_2 as the unstable (positive) root, with corresponding eigenvector $[\phi_2 \ 1]'$. The slopes of the stable and unstable arms of the saddle path are given by the following expressions:

$$\phi_1 = \frac{\sigma(1-b) + \lambda_1}{\sigma a} < 0, \text{ and}$$

$$\phi_2 = \frac{\sigma(1-b) + \lambda_2}{\sigma a} > 0.$$

The initial jump in $q(t)$ at time zero is

$$q(0) - \bar{q}_1 = e^{-\lambda_2 T}\left(d\bar{q} - \phi_1 d\bar{Y}\right)$$

This expression is obviously decreasing in T.

Exercise 6.4

Consider the following partial equilibrium model of investment and capital accumulation, where the discount rate (r) and the depreciation rate (δ) are exogenously given constants. $I(t)$ is the flow rate of gross investment, $K(t)$ is the capital stock and $q(t)$ is the shadow value of capital at time t.

$$\dot{q}(t) = (r+\delta)q(t) - F'[K(t)] + A_K[I(t), K(t)]$$

$$\dot{K}(t) = I(t) - \delta K(t)$$

$$q(t) = A_I[I(t), K(t)]$$

We assume $F'(K) > 0, F''(K) < 0$, and that the function $A(I, K)$, which gives the cost to acquire and install capital, is linearly homogeneous in I and K. We also assume the following signs for the first and second partial derivatives of $A(I, K)$:

$A_I > 0$, $A_{II} > 0$, $A_K < 0$, $A_{KK} > 0$, and $A_{IK} < 0$.

Thus, the firm faces steeply rising investment costs if it invests too rapidly, relative to its existing capital stock.

Derive a linearized dynamic system describing the motion of the capital stock and its shadow value. Demonstrate that the system is stable, and solve the model.

Hint: Use the fact that $A(I, K)$ is linearly homogeneous to simplify the coefficient matrix of the linearized system.

Solution: We assumed that the function $A(I, K)$ is linearly homogeneous in I and K, which implies that its first derivatives are homogeneous of degree zero. Therefore, by Euler's theorem,

$A_{II} I + A_{IK} K = 0$, and $A_{IK} I + A_{KK} K = 0$.

Combine these equations to show that

$$A_{II}A_{KK} - (A_{IK})^2 = 0.$$

The homogeneity of $A(I,K)$ can also be used to show that, near the steady state about which our linear approximation is taken,

$$\delta = -\frac{A_{IK}}{A_{II}}.$$

The linearized dynamic system therefore simplifies to the following matrix equation:

$$\begin{bmatrix} \dot{q}(t) \\ \dot{K}(t) \end{bmatrix} = \begin{bmatrix} r & -F''(\overline{K}) \\ \frac{1}{A_{II}(\overline{I},\overline{K})} & 0 \end{bmatrix} \begin{bmatrix} q(t) - \overline{q} \\ K(t) - \overline{K} \end{bmatrix}$$

$\overline{K}$ is the steady state capital stock, while $\overline{I}$ is the steady state level of gross investment. The system is saddle point stable, since

$$\lambda_1 \lambda_2 = \begin{vmatrix} r & -F''(\overline{K}) \\ \frac{1}{\overline{A}_{II}} & 0 \end{vmatrix} < 0.$$

We can also infer that

$$\lambda_1 + \lambda_1 = tr \begin{bmatrix} r & -F''(\overline{K}) \\ \frac{1}{\overline{A}_{II}} & 0 \end{bmatrix} = r > 0.$$

Let $\lambda_1 < 0$ be the stable root and $\lambda_2 > 0$ be the unstable root, and write the general solution to the system as

$$q(t) = \overline{q} + B_1 \overline{A}_{II} \lambda_1 e^{\lambda_1 t} + B_2 \overline{A}_{II} \lambda_2 e^{\lambda_2 t}$$
$$K(t) = \overline{K} + B_1 e^{\lambda_1 t} + B_2 e^{\lambda_2 t}$$

where B_1 and B_2 are arbitrary constants of integration. Note that the unstable root, λ_2, is greater in absolute value than the stable root, λ_1. This means that the unstable root will dominate, and the solutions for $q(t)$ and $K(t)$ will explode as $t \to \infty$, unless we impose the restriction $B_2 = 0$. Use the initial condition, $K(0) = K_0$ to solve for B_1, leading to the following solution:

$$q(t) = \bar{q} + (K_0 - \bar{K})\bar{A}_{II}\lambda_1 e^{\lambda_1 t}, \text{ and}$$

$$K(t) = \bar{K} + (K_0 - \bar{K})e^{\lambda_1 t}.$$

Exercise 6.5

Analyze the dynamic response to a permanent decrease in the discount rate, r, which is announced and implemented at time $t = 0$. Assume the system is at the steady state point $(\bar{K}_1, \bar{q}_1)$ prior to the announcement, and denote the new steady state by the ordered pair $(\bar{K}_2, \bar{q}_2)$. Use a phase diagram in your analysis, and derive algebraic expressions for the initial jump in $q(t)$ and $I(t)$ at the time of the announcement.

Hint: Use the fact that

$$d\bar{K} \equiv \bar{K}_2 - \bar{K}_1 = \frac{\partial \bar{K}}{\partial r} dr,$$

to express the jumps in $q(t)$ and $I(t)$ as a function of the change in r.

Solution: Using the solution from Exercise 6.4, where we begin at $(\bar{K}_1, \bar{q}_1)$ and eventually end up at $(\bar{K}_2, \bar{q}_2)$, the following equations must be satisfied starting from the time of the announcement:

$$q(t) = \bar{q}_2 + (\bar{K}_1 - \bar{K}_2)A_{II}(\bar{I}_2, \bar{K}_2)\lambda_1 e^{\lambda_1 t}, \text{ and}$$

$$K(t) = \bar{K}_2 + (\bar{K}_1 - \bar{K}_2)e^{\lambda_1 t}.$$

The initial jumps in the shadow value of capital and the rate of gross investment are given by

$$q(0) - \bar{q}_1 = -\frac{\bar{q}_2}{\lambda_2} dr > 0, \text{ and}$$

$$I(0) - \bar{I}_1 = -\frac{1}{A_{II}(\bar{I}_2, \bar{K}_2)} \frac{\bar{q}_2}{\lambda_2} dr > 0,$$

where $dr < 0$ is the change in the discount rate that occurs at time zero. Of course, we should account for the fact that the eigenvalues λ_1 and λ_2 depend on r when analyzing this sort of change, but this would significantly complicate the exercise.

The announcement effect on $q(t)$ is represented as a jump from point 1 to point 2 in the phase diagram below. The system then converges to the new steady state (point 3) along the new stable arm S'S'.

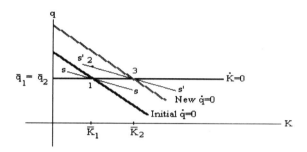

Exercise 6.6

The following model is identical to the exchange rate model presented in Section 6.4 of the text, except the uncovered interest parity condition is relaxed to allow for a premium on the return to foreign bonds, which is proportional to the exchange rate. A depreciation of the domestic currency (increase in E) raises the proportion of the investor's portfolio held in foreign bonds, leading to an increase in the premium. Since it is difficult to interpret a risk premium within the context of a perfect foresight model, you may think of the additional return to foreign bonds as a liquidity premium. The model consists of three equations.

$$R(t) = R*(t) + \dot{E}(t) - \sigma E(t)$$

$$M(t) - P(t) = \alpha_1 Y(t) - \alpha_2 R(t)$$

$$\dot{P}(t) = \rho\left[\beta_0 + (\beta_1 - 1)Y(t) - \beta_2 R(t) + \beta_3(E(t) - P(t))\right]$$

All of the parameters are positive, and we also assume that $0 < \beta_1 < 1$.

Set up and solve the dynamic system governing the evolution of the nominal exchange rate, E, and the price level, P, assuming that E is a "jump" variable and P is a "sluggish" variable. Draw a phase diagram, and explain how it differs from the diagram in Section 6.4 of the text.

Hint: A steady state analysis will add to your understanding of the dynamics of this model.

Solution: The dynamic system may be written in matrix form as follows:

$$\begin{bmatrix} \dot{E}(t) \\ \dot{P}(t) \end{bmatrix} = \begin{bmatrix} \sigma & \dfrac{1}{\alpha_2} \\ \rho\beta_3 & -\rho\left(\beta_3 + \dfrac{\beta_2}{\alpha_2}\right) \end{bmatrix} \begin{bmatrix} E(t) - \overline{E} \\ P(t) - \overline{P} \end{bmatrix}.$$

The general solution to the system is given by:

$$E(t) = \overline{E} + A_1 \frac{1}{\alpha_2(\lambda_1 - \sigma)} e^{\lambda_1 t} + A_2 \frac{1}{\alpha_2(\lambda_2 - \sigma)} e^{\lambda_2 t}, \text{ and}$$

$$P(t) = \overline{P} + A_1 e^{\lambda_1 t} + A_2 e^{\lambda_2 t},$$

where $\lambda_1 < 0$ is the stable root, $\lambda_2 > 0$ is the unstable root, and there are two constants of integration to solve for. While it is not clear which root dominates in the long run (i.e., which root is greater in absolute value), a sufficient condition for stability is to set $A_2 = 0$ and use the initial condition on the price level to solve for $A_1 = P_o - \overline{P}$, leaving the following equations to define the paths of $E(t)$ and $P(t)$ over time.

$$E(t) = \overline{E} + (P_0 - \overline{P}) \frac{1}{\alpha_2(\lambda_1 - \sigma)} e^{\lambda_1 t}$$

$$P(t) = \overline{P} + (P_0 - \overline{P}) e^{\lambda_1 t}$$

The introduction of a premium on foreign bonds results in a downward-sloping $\dot{E} = 0$ locus, as opposed to the horizontal $\dot{E} = 0$ locus found in the version of the exchange rate model presented in Section 6.4 of the text. The phase diagram is shown below.

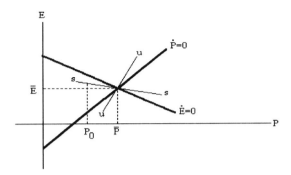

Given the initial price level, P_0, an exchange rate jump must occur, placing the state of the economy onto the SS locus. The system converges to the steady state point $(\overline{P}, \overline{E})$ along the stable arm SS.

Exercise 6.7

Suppose the dynamic system described in Exerçise 6.6 is in long run equilibrium at the point $(\overline{P}_1, \overline{E}_1)$, when it is announced at time $t = 0$ that a permanent increase in the money supply $(dM > 0)$ will be implemented at time $t = T > 0$. This policy change will ultimately force the system to a new steady state point $(\overline{P}_2, \overline{E}_2)$.

Use a phase diagram to depict the dynamic response of the system to this sequence of events. Also, solve for a set of four equations that describe the evolution of $E(t)$ and $P(t)$ during the time periods $0 < t \le T$ and $t \ge T$. Verify that these equations are consistent with your diagram.

Hint: Remember that the steady state loci do not shift until the new policy is implemented at time t=T. Also, to complete the last part of the exercise, it may help to determine which endogenous variable (P or E) changes more in the long run, and to demonstrate that the unstable arm of the saddle path has a slope greater than one.

Solution: The phase diagram shown below depicts the three-phase adjustment process in response to a preannounced, permanent increase in the money supply. First, there is a discrete currency depreciation at the time of the announcement, causing a jump from point 1 to point 2. There is further depreciation and the price level increases as the system evolves along the unstable path from point 2 to point 3, which is reached at time $t = T$. Thereafter, the system evolves along the new stable arm S'S' toward the new steady state $(\overline{P}_2, \overline{E}_2)$ at point 4. Note that the currency is appreciating during this phase, reversing the exchange rate overshooting that occurs during the $0 < t \leq T$ time frame.

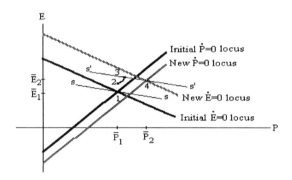

The equations describing this three-phase response to a preannounced increase in the money supply are shown below.

$0 < t \leq T$:

$$E(t) = \overline{E}_1 - e^{-\lambda_2 T}\left(\frac{\lambda_2 - \sigma}{\lambda_1 - \lambda_2}\right)\left[d\overline{E} - \left(\frac{1}{\alpha_2(\lambda_1 - \sigma)}\right)d\overline{P}\right]e^{\lambda_1 t}$$

$$+ e^{-\lambda_2 T}\left(\frac{\lambda_1 - \sigma}{\lambda_1 - \lambda_2}\right)\left[d\overline{E} - \left(\frac{1}{\alpha_2(\lambda_1 - \sigma)}\right)d\overline{P}\right]e^{\lambda_2 t}$$

$$P(t) = \overline{P}_1 - e^{-\lambda_2 T}\left(\frac{\alpha_2(\lambda_2 - \sigma)(\lambda_1 - \sigma)}{\lambda_1 - \lambda_2}\right)\left(e^{\lambda_1 t} - e^{\lambda_2 t}\right)d\overline{E}$$

$$+ e^{-\lambda_2 T}\left(\frac{\alpha_2(\lambda_2 - \sigma)(\lambda_1 - \sigma)}{\lambda_1 - \lambda_2}\right)\left(e^{\lambda_1 t} - e^{\lambda_2 t}\right)\frac{d\overline{P}}{\alpha_2(\lambda_1 - \sigma)}$$

$t \geq T$:

$$E(t) = \overline{E}_2 + e^{\lambda_1 t}\left(\frac{\lambda_2 - \sigma}{\lambda_1 - \lambda_2}\right)\left(e^{-\lambda_1 T} - e^{-\lambda_2 T}\right)d\overline{E}$$

$$- e^{\lambda_1 t}\left(\frac{\lambda_2 - \sigma}{\lambda_1 - \lambda_2}\right)\left[\frac{e^{-\lambda_1 T}}{\alpha_2(\lambda_2 - \sigma)} - \frac{e^{-\lambda_2 T}}{\alpha_2(\lambda_1 - \sigma)}\right]d\overline{P}$$

$$P(t) = \overline{P}_2 + e^{\lambda_1 t}\left(\frac{\alpha_2(\lambda_2 - \sigma)(\lambda_1 - \sigma)}{\lambda_1 - \lambda_2}\right)\left(e^{-\lambda_1 T} - e^{-\lambda_2 T}\right)d\overline{E}$$

$$- e^{\lambda_1 t}\left(\frac{\alpha_2(\lambda_2 - \sigma)(\lambda_1 - \sigma)}{\lambda_1 - \lambda_2}\right)\left[\frac{e^{-\lambda_1 T}}{\alpha_2(\lambda_2 - \sigma)} - \frac{e^{-\lambda_2 T}}{\alpha_2(\lambda_1 - \sigma)}\right]d\overline{P}$$

We can see that these equations are consistent with the phase diagram in several respects. First, the term $e^{\lambda_2 t}$ appears in the first two equations, but not in the latter two. This reflects the fact that there is an unstable component to the system for $0 < t \leq T$, but not for $t \geq T$. Secondly, we can see from the second equation that the price level does not jump at time $t = 0$, since we assumed that $P(0) = P_1$ and $e^0 - e^0 = 1 - 1 = 0$. Finally, one can take time derivatives in each equation and show that $\dot{P} > 0$ for all $t > 0$, while $\dot{E} > 0$ for $0 < t < T$, and $\dot{E} < 0$ for $t > T$. When you attempt to sign these time derivatives, it helps to recall the static result that $d\overline{P} \equiv \overline{P}_2 - \overline{P}_1 > \overline{E}_2 - \overline{E}_1 \equiv d\overline{E}$, and to use the fact that the slope of the unstable arm exceeds unity.

7 The Stability of Government Deficit Financing under Rational Expectations

Exercise 7.1

Bennett T. McCallum developed a perfect foresight model in which a representative household chooses consumption and money holdings each period so as to maximize lifetime utility over an infinite horizon (1984, *Journal of Political Economy*, 92, 123-35). One purpose of the model was to determine whether "a constant, positive government budget deficit can be maintained permanently and without inflation if it is financed by the issue of bonds rather than money." This exercise and the following one are based on portions of McCallum's analysis.

The individual may purchase one period government bonds for Q_t dollars (per bond) at time t and redeem each bond for one dollar the next period. The nominal rate of return on such a bond is given by

$$R_t = \frac{1 - Q_t}{Q_t}.$$

Define the real return, r_t, by the equation

$$1 + r_t = \frac{1 + R_t}{1 + \pi_t} = \frac{1 + R_t}{P_{t+1}/P_t},$$

where P_t is the price level at time t. Let B_t represent the number of bonds acquired at time t and $b_t = B_t/P_t$ represent the face value of those bonds in real terms (i.e., the value in terms of some numeraire consumption good). It turns out that one of the sufficient conditions for the consumer's utility maximization problem is that the present utility value of his bond holdings must go to zero in the limit (see Part III of the text). Mathematically,

$$\lim_{t \to \infty} b_{t+1} \frac{\lambda}{(1+r)^t} = 0,$$

where λ is the marginal value of real income and r is the constant steady state real interest rate. We assume that $r > 0$. Finally, the government budget constraint is given by

$$M_{t+1} - M_t + Q_t B_{t+1} - B_t = P_t(g_t + v_t),$$

where M_t is the nominal money stock at time t (so $m_t \equiv M_t/P_t$ would be the real money stock), g_t represents real government purchases and v_t stands for government transfer payments net of any tax revenue.

Demonstrate that a permanent, constant government budget deficit $(d \equiv g + v)$, that is completely bond financed, must violate the sufficient condition for lifetime utility maximization given above.

Hint: Impose zero money growth and convert the government budget constraint to real terms. Assume that $r_t \to r$ and $(g_t + v_t) \to d$ in the long run.

Solution: Once the economy has converged to its steady state, the real stock of government bonds continues to evolve according to the following difference equation:

$$b_{t+1} = (1+r)b_t + (1+r)d, \quad t = 1, 2, \ldots$$

While this process is clearly unstable, that does not necessarily mean that the present utility value of the stock of real bonds is growing without bound. By recursive substitution, we find that

$$b_{t+1} = (1+r)^t b_1 + (1+r)d\left[1 + (1+r) + \ldots + (1+r)^{t-1}\right],$$

which implies that

$$b_{t+1} \frac{\lambda}{(1+r)^t} = \lambda b_1 + \frac{\lambda d\left[(1+r) - (1+r)^{1-t}\right]}{r} \xrightarrow[t \to \infty]{} \lambda b_1 + \frac{\lambda d(1+r)}{r} > 0.$$

The consumer's optimality condition is violated by ongoing bond-financed deficits in this form.

Exercise 7.2

Using the model presented in Exercise 7.1, show that a constant bond-financed deficit can be sustained indefinitely, without violating the sufficient condition for utility maximization, if we redefine the deficit to include current interest payments.

Hint: Use the nominal government budget constraint, under the assumption of no money growth, to derive an expression for $\tilde{B}_{t+1} - \tilde{B}_t$, where

$$\tilde{B}_t \equiv \frac{B_t}{1+R_{t-1}} \quad, and \quad \tilde{B}_{t+1} \equiv \frac{B_{t+1}}{1+R_t}.$$

Assume that fiscal policy is set so as to hold the real value of $\tilde{B}_{t+1} - \tilde{B}_t$ constant over time.

Solution: The government budget constraint is

$$\tilde{B}_{t+1} - \tilde{B}_t = P_t(g_t + v_t) + \tilde{B}_t R_{t-1},$$

and we assume this expression for the deficit is held constant in real terms, at some level $\tilde{d} > 0$, which simplifies the fiscal constraint to

$$\tilde{B}_{t+1} - \tilde{B}_t = \tilde{d} P_t.$$

We consider a steady state situation, where the price level and the real interest rate are constant over time. In steady state, the following difference equation defines the evolution of the real stock of bonds:

$$b_{t+1} - b_t = d(1+r).$$

By recursive substitution, we find that

$$b_{t+1} = b_1 + \tilde{d}\, t(1+r),$$

so that

$$b_{t+1} \frac{\lambda}{(1+r)^t} = \frac{\lambda b_1 + \lambda \tilde{d}\, t(1+r)}{(1+r)^t} \xrightarrow[t \to \infty]{} 0.$$

This expression goes to zero as t becomes arbitrarily large, because the numerator grows as a linear function of t, while the denominator grows much more rapidly as an exponential function of t. We conclude that a constant real deficit may be consistent with lifetime utility maximization, so long as we include the real interest payments associated with current borrowing in our definition of the deficit. We should point out that McCallum checks to make sure that all consumer optimality conditions are satisfied in this long run equilibrium; not just the sufficient condition emphasized in this exercise.

Exercise 7.3

William Scarth analyzes the stability of bond financed deficits in the context of the following model (1980, *Economics Letters*, v. 6, pp. 321-27):

$$Y_t = d_1\overline{Y} - d_2 r_t + d_3(E_t P_{t+1} - P_t) + d_4(\overline{M} - P_t) + d_5 B_t + G_t + u_{1t}$$

$$\overline{M} - P_t = \alpha_1\overline{Y} - \alpha_2 r_t + \alpha_3 B_t + u_{2t}$$

$$P = \gamma\left[(Y_t - \overline{Y})/\overline{Y}\right] + E_{t-1}P_t + u_{3t}$$

$$G_t = k\overline{Y} + (1-k)\overline{B}$$

$$B_{t+1} - B_t = -k\overline{r}(Y_t - \overline{Y}) + (1-k)\overline{r}B_t - \overline{B}(P_{t+1} - P_t)$$

All coefficients are assumed to be positive, with d_1 and k further assumed to be positive fractions. Over-bars indicate steady state values. The tax rate is given by k, and the five endogenous variables are denoted in the usual way (P, Y, r, B, G). Government bonds are consols, so that B_t represents both the quantity of bonds and the interest payment due at time t.

Solve the model for a reduced form stochastic difference equation describing the evolution of the price level, P_t.

Hint: Try eliminating variables through substitutions in the following order: G_t, r_t, Y_t, $B_{t+1} - B_t$, and finally B_t. Needless to say, the algebra is fairly tedious.

Solution: The reduced form stochastic difference equation for P_t takes the form

$$P_t = h_1 P_{t-1} + h_2 E_{t-1} P_t + h_3 E_t P_{t+1} + h_4 E_{t-2} P_{t-1} + \theta + v_t,$$

where:

Solve for a reduced form stochastic process for P_t that satisfies this difference equation, using the method of undetermined coefficients.

Hint: Postulate a solution of the form

$$P_t = \overline{P} + \sum_{i=0}^{\infty} \lambda_i v_{t-i},$$

where $\overline{P}$ *and* λ_i $(i = 0,1,2,...)$ *are the coefficients to be determined, if possible.*

Solution: We find that λ_0 is indeterminate, while

$$\overline{P} = \theta/(1 - h_1 - h_2 - h_3 - h_4),$$

and the remaining coefficients must satisfy the following restrictions:

$$\lambda_0 = 1 + h_3 \lambda_1,$$

$$(1 - h_2)\lambda_1 = h_1 \lambda_0 + h_3 \lambda_2, \text{ and}$$

$$\lambda_{i+2} = \left(\frac{1 - h_2}{h_3}\right) \lambda_{i+1} - \left(\frac{h_1 + h_4}{h_3}\right) \lambda_i. \qquad (i = 1, 2, 3,...)$$

Exercise 7.5

Using the results from the previous two exercises, show that there is no stable solution for P_t, if we assume that $\alpha_3 \overline{B} < 1$ and $d_5 k \overline{r} < 1$. Scarth argues that these asumptions, which place an upper limit on the wealth effect that a change in the stock of government bonds has on the IS and LM curves, are very plausible.

Hint: Given the assumptions that $\alpha_3 \overline{B} < 1$ *and* $d_5 k \overline{r} < 1$, *one can show that* h_1 *must be positive.*

Solution: One way to ensure stability is to set $\lambda_1 = \lambda_2 = \cdots = 0$. However, with $h_1 > 0$, this implies two different values for λ_0: $\lambda_0 = 1$ and $\lambda_0 = 0$. Thus, we are forced to consider nontrivial solutions. Nontrivial solutions for P_t are stable only if the second order difference equation for the undeter-

$$h_1 = \frac{1}{A}\left[(1+\bar{r}(1-k))\left(1+\frac{\phi\gamma}{\bar{Y}}\right)+\psi k\bar{r}-\gamma\psi\frac{\bar{B}}{\bar{Y}}\right],$$

$$h_2 = \frac{1}{A}\left[1-\gamma d_3\frac{1+\bar{r}(1-k)}{\bar{Y}}\right],$$

$$h_3 = \frac{1}{A}\left[\frac{\gamma d_3}{\bar{Y}}\right],$$

$$h_4 = -\frac{1}{A}\left[\psi k\bar{r}+1+\bar{r}(1-k)\right],$$

$$A = 1+\frac{\phi\gamma}{\bar{Y}}-\gamma\psi\frac{\bar{B}}{\bar{Y}},$$

$$\phi = d_3 + d_4 + \frac{d_2}{\alpha_2},$$

$$\psi = \frac{d_2\alpha_3}{\alpha_2} - d_5,$$

$$\theta = \frac{\gamma\bar{r}(1-k)}{A}\left[(1-k-d_1)+\frac{\alpha_1 d_2}{\alpha_2}-\left(\frac{d_2}{\alpha_2}+d_4\right)\frac{\bar{M}}{\bar{Y}}-(1-k)\frac{\bar{B}}{\bar{Y}}\right],$$

$$v_t = \frac{1}{A}\left[w_t - (1+\bar{r}(1-k))w_{t-1} - \psi k\bar{r}u_{3t-1}\right], \text{ and}$$

$$w_t = u_{3t} + \frac{\gamma}{\bar{Y}}\left(u_{1t} - \frac{d_2}{\alpha_2}u_{2t}\right).$$

Exercise 7.4

In Exercise 7.3, we derived the following stochastic difference equation for the price level:

$$P_t = h_1 P_{t-1} + h_2 E_{t-1} P_t + h_3 E_t P_{t+1} + h_4 E_{t-2} P_{t-1} + \theta + v_t.$$

mined coefficients is convergent. Recall the difference equation from Exercise 7.4:

$$\lambda_{i+2} = \left(\frac{1-h_2}{h_3}\right)\lambda_{i+1} - \left(\frac{h_1+h_4}{h_3}\right)\lambda_i \qquad (i=1,2,3,\ldots).$$

A necessary condition for this process to be stable is that

$$\frac{h_1+h_4}{h_3} < 1.$$

Using the expressions for h_1, h_3 and h_4 derived in Exercise 7.3, we can show that

$$\frac{h_1+h_4}{h_3} = 1 + \bar{r}(1-k) + \frac{d_4}{d_3} + \frac{d_2}{\alpha_2 d_3}(1-\alpha_3\bar{B}) + \frac{d_5}{d_3}\bar{B} + \left(d_4 + \frac{d_2}{\alpha_2}\right)\frac{\bar{r}(1-k)}{d_3}$$

Since $0 < k < 1$, and we have assumed that $\alpha_3\bar{B} < 1$, we can conclude that

$$\frac{h_1+h_4}{h_3} > 1.$$

Thus, there are no stable processes for P_t that satisfy the model outlined in Exercise 7.3.

Exercise 7.6

In his 1987 article, "Can Economic Growth Make Monetarist Arithmetic Pleasant?" (*Southern Economic Journal*, 53, 1028-36), William Scarth analyzes the relative merits of money and bond financing of government deficits, in the context of a growing economy. He begins with the following continuous time representation of the government budget constraint:

$$G(t) + (1-k)B(t) - kY(t) = \frac{\dot{M}(t)}{P(t)} + \frac{\dot{B}(t)}{r(t)},$$

where:

$G(t) \quad \equiv \quad$ real government expenditures,

Chapter 7

$B(t) \equiv$ real interest payments on government bonds,

$Y(t) \equiv$ real output,

$M(t) \equiv$ the nominal money stock,

$r(t) \equiv$ the real interest rate, and

$k \equiv$ the proportional tax rate $(0 < k < 1)$.

The bonds are assumed to be consols, so that $B(t)$ also represents the quantity of bonds outstanding at time t.

Let N denote the natural rate of output, and assume it grows exogenously at the fixed rate $n \equiv \dot{N}/N$. Divide through the government budget constraint by N, and rewrite the equation so that the only time derivatives are $\dot{L}$ and $\dot{D}$, where

$$L \equiv \frac{M}{PN} \equiv \text{real liquidity relative to } N, \text{ and}$$

$$D \equiv \frac{B}{N} \equiv \text{real government debt relative to } N.$$

Also, let $y \equiv Y/N$, $g \equiv G/N$ and $\pi \equiv \dot{P}/P$. Take a linear approximation to the resulting equation about the steady state $(\bar{r}, \bar{\pi}, \bar{L}, \bar{D})$, treating n, k and g as exogenously given constants. Finally, rewrite the approximate government budget constraint in discrete time for the case of all money financing $(\dot{D} = 0)$ and also for the case of all bond financing $(\dot{L} = 0)$.

Hint: The inflation rate from t-1 to t may be approximated as $\pi_t = p_t - p_{t-1}$, where $p_t \equiv \ln(P_t)$.

Solution: After dividing through by N and using the quotient rule to compute

$$\dot{L} \equiv \frac{d}{dt}\left(\frac{M}{PN}\right) \text{ and } \dot{D} \equiv \frac{d}{dt}\left(\frac{B}{N}\right),$$

we arrive at the following continuous time government budget constraint in "growth form:"

$$\dot{L} + \left(\frac{1}{r}\right)\dot{D} = g + (1-k)D - ky - (n+\pi)L - D\left(\frac{n}{r}\right).$$

A linear approximation near steady state to this nonlinear equation is

$$\dot{L} + \left(\frac{1}{\bar{r}}\right)\dot{D} = g + \left(1 - k - \frac{n}{\bar{r}}\right)D - ky - (n + \bar{\pi})L - \bar{L}\pi + ar + x,$$

where $a \equiv \dfrac{n\overline{D}}{\bar{r}^2}$ and $x \equiv \bar{L}\bar{\pi} - \dfrac{n\overline{D}}{\bar{r}}$.

Now, the time derivative of some general function Z(t) is given by

$$\dot{Z}(t) \equiv \lim_{\Delta t \to 0} \frac{Z(t + \Delta t) - Z(t)}{\Delta t}.$$

However, if Z(t) is a linear function, we can arbitrarily choose a unit interval by setting $\Delta t = 1$ and writing the definition of the time derivative of Z(t) as

$$\dot{Z}(t) \equiv Z(t+1) - Z(t) \equiv Z_{t+1} - Z_t.$$

We make use of this approximation to rewrite the government budget constraint in discrete time under the different financing regimes.

$$L_t = (1 - n - \bar{\pi})L_{t-1} + g - ky_{t-1} - \bar{L}(p_t - p_{t-1}) + ar_{t-1}$$
$$+ x + \frac{[\bar{r}(1-k) - n]\overline{D}}{\bar{r}}$$

$$D_t = [1 + \bar{r}(1-k) - n]D_{t-1} + \bar{r}g - \bar{r}ky_{t-1} - \bar{r}\bar{L}(p_t - p_{t-1})$$
$$+ a\bar{r}r_{t-1} + \bar{r}x - \bar{r}(n + \bar{\pi})\bar{L}$$

The first equation reflects all money finance $(\dot{D} = 0)$, while the second equation assumes that deficits are financed with bonds only $(\dot{L} = 0)$.

Exercise 7.7

An apparent implication of the expression for the ratio of bonds to the natural rate of output (D_t) derived in Exercise 7.6 is that D_t will converge to a finite steady state level if $n > \bar{r}(1-k)$. However, we must also take into account any systematic movements in output, inflation and the interest rate. To illustrate the importance of these considerations, suppose the interest rate remains constant, inflation follows the exogenously given autoregressive process

$$\pi_t = (1-\phi)\mu + \phi\pi_{t-1} + \varepsilon_t,$$

and output is determined by the aggregate demand equation specified by Scarth in his 1987 article:

$$y_t = b\overline{L} + cD_t + dg - ek + f E_{t-1}(p_{t+1} - p_t) + Z + u_t.$$

Assume that ε_t and u_t are mutually uncorrelated, zero mean, white noise error terms. Determine the conditions under which D_t and $\pi_t \equiv p_t - p_{t-1}$ converge to finite steady state values.

Hint: Since we are treating the inflation process as exogenously given, we can write the solution for D_t as a function of π_t. Of course, this sort of expression is obviously not a general equilibrium solution in any realistic sense.

Solution: The condition for a stable inflation rate process is $|\phi| < 1$. Assuming this condition is satisfied, the process for D_t will be stable if $n > \bar{r}[1 - (1+c)k]$, since we find that

$$\begin{aligned}D_t = \psi &+ \{1 + \bar{r}[1-(1+c)k] - n\}D_{t-1} - \bar{r}ku_{t-1} \\ &- \bar{r}(fk + \overline{L})\pi_t + \bar{r}fk(\varepsilon_t + \phi\varepsilon_{t-1})\end{aligned},$$

where

$$\psi \equiv \bar{r}(g - n\overline{L}) - \bar{r}k(b\overline{L} + dg - ek + z).$$

If we want to trace the effects of the underlying inflation shocks on D_t, we can substitute the infinite moving average (Wold) form of the process for π_t into the above equation. Specifically, we would substitute the expression

$$\pi_t = \mu + \sum_{i=0}^{\infty} \phi^i \varepsilon_{t-i}$$

into the solution for D_t.

8 Macroeconomic Stabilization Policy under Rational Expectations

Exercise 8.1

This exercise continues the analysis of Scarth's model, which was started in Exercises 7.6 and 7.7. We add a process for $\bar{y}_t \equiv \bar{Y}_t/N_t$, where $\bar{Y}_t$ is the so-called "full information" level of output that would occur if there were no expectational errors. We also add the aggregate supply function, which is due to McCallum (1980, *Journal of Money, Credit and Banking*, 12, 714-746). Overall, the model consists of the following equations:

$$L_t = (1-n-\bar{\pi})L_{t-1} + g - k y_{t-1} - \bar{L}(p_t - p_{t-1}) + ar_{t-1}$$
$$+ x + \frac{[\bar{r}(1-k)-n]\bar{D}}{\bar{r}}$$

$$D_t = [1+\bar{r}(1-k)-n]D_{t-1} + \bar{r}g - \bar{r}k y_{t-1} - \bar{r}\bar{L}(p_t - p_{t-1})$$
$$+ a\bar{r}r_{t-1} + \bar{r}x - \bar{r}(n+\bar{\pi})\bar{L}$$

$$y_t = bL_t + cD_t + dg - ek + f E_{t-1}(p_{t+1} - p_t) + z + u_t$$

$$\bar{y}_t = 1 + v_t$$

$$p_t - p_{t-1} = E_{t-1}(\bar{p}_t) - \bar{p}_{t-1} + \theta(y_{t-1} - \bar{y}_{t-1})$$

All coefficients are strictly positive, and the error terms u_t and v_t are assumed to be mutually uncorrelated. By definition, $\bar{p}_t$ is the value of p_t that makes $y_t = \bar{y}_t$. Note that the last equation implies that p_t is predetermined, in the sense that $E_{t-1}p_t = p_t$. Finally, to analyze the effects of money-financing, replace the second equation by $D_t = \bar{D}$, and to analyze the effects of bond-financing, replace the first equation by $L_t = \bar{L}$.

Define deviations from full information output (in proportion to N_t) with the variable $\hat{y}_t \equiv y_t - \bar{y}_t$. Derive an ARMA (Autoregressive Moving Average) equation for $\hat{y}_t$ under both deficit financing policies (all money-financing and all bond-financing). Compute the unconditional variance of deviations from capacity output $\left(\sigma_{\hat{y}}^2 \equiv var(\hat{y}_t)\right)$ for each policy extreme, and determine a sufficient condition for $\sigma_{\hat{y}}^2$ to be smaller under money-financing.

Hint: Combine the government budget constraint and the aggregate demand equation, and solve for p_t, recalling that the price level is predetermined. By definition, $\bar{p}_t$ obeys the same equation, except that y_t is replaced by $\bar{y}_t$.

Solution: We find that

$$\hat{y}_t = (1-\theta\gamma)\hat{y}_{t-1} + u_t - v_t,$$

where $\gamma = b\bar{L} + f$ for money-financed deficits, while $\gamma = cr\bar{L} + f$ for bond-financed deficits. The unconditional variance of deviations of y_t from $\bar{y}_t$ is given by

$$\sigma_{\hat{y}}^2 = \frac{\sigma_u^2 + \sigma_v^2}{1-(1-\theta\gamma)^2}.$$

So long as $0 < \theta\gamma < 2$, $\sigma_{\hat{y}}^2$ will be finite. Money financing results in a lower value for $\sigma_{\hat{y}}^2$ if $b > c\bar{r}$, and Scarth argues that this condition is almost certainly satisfied.

Exercise 8.2

Exercise 8.1 assumed deficits are completely financed by either money or bonds. Suppose there were a mixture of money and bond financing. Specifically, assume a fixed ratio between the stock of real bonds and the stock of real money:

$$\frac{D_t}{L_t} \equiv \frac{B_t/N_t}{M_t/(P_tN_t)} = \frac{B_t}{(M_t/P_t)} = \lambda \quad \forall t.$$

Derive an expression for $\sigma_{\hat{y}}^2$ and determine the value of λ that satisfies the first order condition for minimizing $\sigma_{\hat{y}}^2$. Discuss the conditions under which this value of λ truly minimizes $\sigma_{\hat{y}}^2$. Obviously, in order to have a nontrivial mixture of money and bond financing, it must be the case that $0 < \lambda < \infty$. Is it possible that the $\sigma_{\hat{y}}^2$ could be made smaller by a policy of either all money financing $(\lambda = 0)$ or all bond financing $(\lambda \to \infty)$? In answering these questions, assume that $c > 0$ and $b > c\bar{r}$.

Hint: Before doing this analysis, you must derive an integrated government budget constraint, that imposes neither $\dot{D} = 0$ nor $\dot{L} = 0$. Start from the linearized, continuous time government budget constraint derived in Exercise 7.6.

Solution: The linearized, discrete time government budget constraint, which has the fixed bonds-to-money ratio, λ, imposed upon it is given below.

$$L_t = \left\{1 - n + \frac{\bar{r}\left[(1-k)\lambda - \bar{\pi}\right]}{\bar{r} + \lambda}\right\} L_{t-1} + \frac{\bar{r}}{\bar{r} + \lambda}\left\{k y_{t-1} - \bar{L}(p_t - p_{t-1}) + a r_{t-1} + g + x\right\}$$

Proceeding as in Exercise 8.1, we derive a dynamic equation for $\hat{y}_t \equiv y_t - \bar{y}_t$:

$$\hat{y}_t = \left[1 - \frac{\theta}{\psi(\lambda)}\right]\hat{y}_{t-1} + u_t - v_t,$$

where $\psi(\lambda) \equiv \dfrac{\bar{r} + \lambda}{f(\bar{r} + \lambda) + \bar{r}\bar{L}(b + c\lambda)} > 0$.

The process for $\hat{y}_t$ is stable so long as $0 < \theta/\psi(\lambda) < 2$. Since θ and $\psi(\lambda)$ are each positive, the stability requirement is simply $\psi(\lambda) > \theta/2$. The variance of $\hat{y}_t$, which will be finite if this condition is satisfied, is given by:

$$\sigma_{\hat{y}}^2 = \frac{\sigma_u^2 + \sigma_v^2}{1 - \left[1 - \dfrac{\theta}{\psi(\lambda)}\right]^2}.$$

We can differentiate the expression for $\sigma_{\hat{y}}^2$ with respect to λ, and, so long as $c > 0$ and $b > c\bar{r}$, the first order condition to minimize $\sigma_{\hat{y}}^2$ is simply to set $\psi(\lambda) = \theta$. This makes intuitive sense, since it reduces the dynamic process for $\hat{y}_t$ to white noise. However, it is not necessarily feasible to set $\psi(\lambda) = \theta$, since this implies

$$\lambda = -\bar{r}\frac{\left[1 - \theta(b\bar{L} + f)\right]}{\left[1 - \theta(cr\bar{L} + f)\right]} \begin{array}{c}>\\<\end{array} 0.$$

Thus, the programming rule to minimize $\sigma_{\hat{y}}^2$ over the feasible domain, $\lambda \geq 0$, is to set

$$\lambda = max\left\{0, -\bar{r}\frac{\left[1-\theta(b\bar{L}+f)\right]}{\left[1-\theta(cr\bar{L}+f)\right]}\right\}.$$

Exercise 8.3

The following model, which is taken from Turnovsky's 1980 article, "The Choice of Monetary Instruments Under Alternative Forms of Price Expectations" (*The Manchester School*, 48, 39-63), is very similar to the model presented in Section 8.2 of the text. The main difference is that, rather than using the Lucas aggregate supply function, this model assumes an expectations-augmented Phillips curve with a unitary expectations coefficient. In addition to the supply function, there are stochastic IS and LM relations, for a total of three equations.

$$y_t = d_1 y_t + d_2\left[r_t - \left(p^*_{t+1,t} - p_t\right)\right] + G + u_{1t} \qquad 0 < d_1 < 1, d_2 < 0$$

$$m_t - p_t = \alpha_1 y_t + \alpha_2 r_t + u_{2t} \qquad \alpha_1 > 0, \alpha_2 < 0$$

$$p_t - p_{t-1} = \gamma(y_t - \bar{y}) + p^*_{t,t-1} - p_{t-1} + u_{3t} \qquad \gamma > 0$$

For the purposes of this exercise, we assume expectations are rational, so $p^*_{t+j,t} \equiv E_t(p_{t+j})$. The error terms have zero mean and are serially uncorrelated, and they have variances denoted by $\sigma_i^2 \equiv E(u_{it}^2); i = 1, 2, 3$. The only nonzero contemporaneous correlation is between u_{1t} and u_{2t}, and it is denoted as $\sigma_{12} \equiv E(u_{1t}u_{2t})$.

Suppose the central bank sets monetary policy so as to peg the nominal interest rate at the constant level $\bar{r}$. Use the IS and Phillips curve equations to solve for a stochastic difference equation governing the evolution of the price level under this policy regime. Apply the method of undetermined coefficients to solve this difference equation, and show that the equilibrium price level is indeterminate, even after imposing stability by setting one of the undetermined coefficients equal to zero. Finally, derive expressions for the unconditional variance of the price level and real output.

Hint: After deriving the stochastic difference equation for p_t, postulate a solution of the form

$$p_t = \bar{p} + \lambda t + \sum_{i=0}^{\infty} \delta_i v_{t-i},$$

where v_t is some composite of the error terms in the model and λ represents the deterministic trend in the price level (to be determined as a function of model parameters, if possible).

Solution: The stochastic difference equation for p_t may be written as

$$d_2\gamma(E_t p_{t+1} - p_t) + (1-d_1)(p_t - E_{t-1}p_t) + \gamma\beta = v_t,$$

where:

$$\beta \equiv [(1-d_1)\bar{y} - d_2\bar{r} - G] \quad \text{and} \quad v_t \equiv \gamma u_{1t} + (1-d_1)u_{3t}.$$

Our "guess" at the form of the solution is

$$p_t = \bar{p} + \lambda t + \sum_{i=0}^{\infty} \delta_i v_{t-i},$$

with $\bar{p}$, λ and the $\delta_i's$ to be determined. The following parameter restrictions must be satisfied by any rational expectations solution for p_t:

$$\lambda = -\frac{\beta}{d_2},$$

$$\delta_0 = \frac{1 - d_2\gamma\delta_1}{1 - d_1 - d_2\gamma}, \text{ and}$$

$$d_2\gamma(\delta_{i+1} - \delta_i) = 0 \quad (i = 1, 2, \cdots).$$

The last restriction implies that

$$\delta_1 = \delta_2 = \cdots = \bar{\delta},$$

resulting in the following solution for p_t:

$$p_t = \bar{p} - \frac{\beta}{d_2}t + \frac{1 - d_2\gamma\bar{\delta}}{1 - d_1 - d_2\gamma}v_t + \bar{\delta}\sum_{i=1}^{\infty} v_{t-i}.$$

Clearly, the only value for $\bar{\delta}$ that results in a finite asymptotic variance for the price level is $\bar{\delta} = 0$. By imposing this restriction, we simplify the solution to

$$p_t = \bar{p} - \frac{\beta}{d_2}t + \frac{v_t}{1 - d_1 - d_2\gamma},$$

which has unconditional variance

$$\sigma_p^2(\bar{r}) = \frac{\gamma^2\sigma_1^2 + (1-d_1)^2\sigma_3^2}{(1-d_1-d_2\gamma)^2}.$$

The functional notation indicates that this variance is associated with a policy of pegging the nominal interest rate. Note that the price level is not uniquely determined, since we are unable to pin down a specific value for the coefficient $\bar{p}$. Finally, by going back to the aggregate supply equation, we can solve for y_t and then compute its unconditional variance.

$$y_t = \bar{y} + \frac{u_{1t} + d_2 u_{3t}}{1 - d_1 - d_2\gamma}$$

$$\sigma_y^2(\bar{r}) = \frac{\sigma_1^2 + d_2^2\sigma_3^2}{(1-d_1-d_2\gamma)^2}$$

Exercise 8.4

Repeat the analysis of Exercise 8.3 under the assumption that the central bank pegs the real interest rate, $k_t \equiv r_t - (E_t p_{t+1} - p_t)$, at the constant level $\bar{k}$. Use Taylor's criterion of minimizing the unconditional variance of the endogenous variable (p_t in this instance) to restrict the values of any indeterminate coefficients. Compare the variances associated with this policy ($\sigma_p^2(\bar{k})$ and $\sigma_y^2(\bar{k})$) to those associated with pegging the nominal interest rate ($\sigma_p^2(\bar{r})$ and $\sigma_y^2(\bar{r})$).

Hint: Taking G and $\bar{y}$ as exogenously given, there is only one value of $\bar{k}$ that admits rational expectations solutions to the model. Impose this restriction before proceeding with the method of undetermined coefficients.

Solution: By imposing $r_t - (E_t p_{t+1} - p_t) = \bar{k}$ on the IS equation, solving this equation for y_t, and substituting the result into the aggregate supply equation, we arrive at the following stochastic difference equation for p_t:

$$(1-d_1)(p_t - E_{t-1}p_t) = \psi + v_t,$$

where

$$\psi \equiv \gamma\left[d_2 \bar{k} + G - (1-d_1)\bar{y}\right].$$

The rational expectations hypothesis requires forecasting errors to be white noise, which means $\psi = 0$ must hold here. This restriction dictates that $\bar{k} = (1/d_2)\left[(1-d_1)\bar{y} - G\right]$. The solutions that satisfy this restriction are of the form:

$$p_t = \bar{p} + \frac{v_t}{1-d_1} + \sum_{i=1}^{\infty} \mu_i v_{t-i},$$

where $\bar{p}$ and μ_i $(i = 1, 2, \cdots)$ are undetermined. While $\sigma_p^2(\bar{k})$ is bounded so long as $\sum_{i=1}^{\infty} \mu_i^2 < \infty$, we impose the restrictions $\mu_1 = \mu_2 = \cdots = 0$ so as to minimize $\sigma_p^2(\bar{k})$, in accordance with Taylor's criterion. This leaves us with the following results:

$$p_t = \bar{p} + \frac{v_t}{1-d_1},$$

$$\sigma_p^2(\bar{k}) = \frac{\gamma^2 \sigma_1^2 + (1-d_1)^2 \sigma_3^2}{(1-d_1)^2},$$

$$y_t = \bar{y} + \frac{u_{1t}}{1-d_1}, \text{ and}$$

$$\sigma_y^2(\bar{k}) = \frac{\sigma_1^2}{(1-d_1)^2}.$$

As in the case of $r_t = \bar{r}$, the price level is indeterminate, but the relevant unconditional variances are bounded.

Recalling that $d_2 < 0$, we can immediately see that $\sigma_p^2(\bar{k}) > \sigma_p^2(\bar{r})$. The relationship between $\sigma_y^2(\bar{k})$ and $\sigma_y^2(\bar{r})$ is not so clear cut. The current policy $(k_t = \bar{k})$ completely insulates output from supply shocks, but volatility of output due to a given sequence of demand (IS and/or LM) shocks is greater than under the fixed nominal rate policy.

Exercise 8.5

Repeat the analysis of Exercise 8.3 once more, assuming the central bank fixes the nominal money stock (i.e., sets $m_t = \overline{m} \ \forall t$). Compare the variance of prices and output, due to both demand and supply disturbances, to the corresponding components of $\sigma_p^2(\overline{r})$ and $\sigma_y^2(\overline{r})$.

Hint: The mean price level is uniquely determined in this case. In fact, there is only one rational expectations solution for p_t that results in a finite unconditional variance $\left(\sigma_p^2(\overline{m}) < \infty\right)$.

Solution: The stochastic difference equation for the price level is

$$Jp_t - HE_{t-1}p_t - \gamma\alpha_2 d_2 E_t p_{t+1} + \gamma\theta = \omega_t,$$

where:

$$H \equiv -\alpha_2(1-d_1) - \alpha_1 d_2 > 0,$$

$$J \equiv H - \gamma d_2(1-\alpha_2) > 0,$$

$$\theta \equiv d_2\overline{m} + H\overline{y} + \alpha_2 G, \text{ and}$$

$$\omega_t \equiv -\gamma\alpha_2 u_{1t} + \gamma d_2 u_{2t} + Hu_{3t}.$$

The general solution for p_t is

$$p_t = \frac{\theta}{d_2} + \left(\frac{1+\gamma\alpha_2 d_2 \delta_1}{J}\right)\omega_t + \delta_1 \sum_{i=1}^{\infty}\left(\frac{1-\alpha_2}{-\alpha_2}\right)^{i-1} \omega_{t-i},$$

where δ_1 is undetermined. However, recall that $\alpha_2 < 0$, so that

$$\frac{1-\alpha_2}{-\alpha_2} > 1.$$

Therefore, we set $\delta_1 = 0$ to bound the unconditional variance of p_t. This leads to the following results:

$$p_t = \frac{\theta}{d_2} + \frac{\omega_t}{J},$$

$$\sigma_p^2(\overline{m}) = \frac{\gamma^2\left[\alpha_2^2\sigma_1^2 + d_2^2\sigma_2^2 - 2\alpha_2 d_2\sigma_{12}\right] + \left[(1-d_1)\alpha_2 + \alpha_1 d_2\right]^2\sigma_3^2}{\left\{\alpha_2(1-d_1) + d_2\left[\alpha_1 + \gamma(1-\alpha_2)\right]\right\}^2},$$

$$y_t = \overline{y} + \frac{-\alpha_2 u_{1t} + d_2 u_{2t} + d_2(1-\alpha_2)u_{3t}}{J}, \text{ and}$$

$$\sigma_y^2(\overline{m}) = \frac{\left[\alpha_2^2\sigma_1^2 + d_2^2\sigma_2^2 - 2\alpha_2 d_2\sigma_{12}\right] + d_2^2(1-\alpha_2)^2\sigma_3^2}{\left\{\alpha_2(1-d_1) + d_2\left[\alpha_1 + \gamma(1-\alpha_2)\right]\right\}^2}.$$

By comparing these results to those found in Exercise 8.3, we conclude that pegging the nominal interest rate is superior to fixing the money stock, if there are no supply shocks and LM shocks "sufficiently dominate" IS shocks. It is more difficult to rank the desirability of these two policies with respect to supply shocks, since the policy that results in the lower output volatility will produce greater price volatility, and vice versa.

Exercise 8.6

The following model is taken from Section III of the 1980 article by Turnovsky, which is referenced in Exercise 8.3. A comparison of monetary instruments is still the subject of analysis, but the rational expectations hypothesis is replaced by the assumption that inflationary expectations are formed autoregressively. The model consists of the five equations below, where the actual rate of inflation from $t-1$ to t is denoted by q_t, while the expectation at time $t-1$ of inflation from $t-1$ to t is denoted by π_t.

$$y_t = d_1 y_t + d_2\left[r_t - (\pi_{t+1})\right] + G + u_{1t} \qquad 0 < d_1 < 1, d_2 < 0$$

$$m_t - p_t = \alpha_1 y_t + \alpha_2 r_t + u_{2t} \qquad \alpha_1 > 0, \alpha_2 < 0$$

$$p_t - p_{t-1} = q_t$$

$$q_t = \gamma(y_t - \overline{y}) + \pi_t + u_{3t} \qquad \gamma > 0$$

$$\pi_{t+1} - \pi_t = \rho(q_t - \pi_t) \qquad 0 < \rho < 1$$

We assume there is some positive nominal interest rate, $\overline{r}$, which permits natural rate output $(y_t = \overline{y})$ to be sustained without generating inflationary expectations. Mathematically, these values are related by the equation

$$(1-d_1)\bar{y} = d_2\bar{r} + G.$$

Derive a stochastic difference equation for the actual inflation rate, which is driven by the stochastic shock terms in the model and deviations of r_t from $\bar{r}$. Show that if $\rho > 0$, and we assume that

$$1 + \frac{d_2\rho\gamma}{1-d_1} > 0$$

(which ensures that positive IS shocks cause a short run increase in output), then a policy of pegging the nominal interest rate results in an unstable stochastic process for the actual rate of inflation.

Hint: Use the first equation in the model and the relationship between $\bar{y}$ and $\bar{r}$ to derive an expression for $y_t - \bar{y}$, which you can substitute into the Phillips curve equation.

Solution: The stochastic difference equation for q_t is

$$\left[1 + \frac{d_2\rho\gamma}{1-d_1}\right]q_t - q_{t-1} = \frac{d_2\gamma}{1-d_1}\left[r'_t - (1-\rho)r'_{t-1}\right] + \frac{\gamma}{1-d_1}\left[u_{1t} - (1-\rho)u_{1t-1}\right]$$
$$+ \left[u_{3t} - (1-\rho)u_{3t-1}\right]$$

where $r'_t \equiv r_t - \bar{r}$. Given the assumptions that we made at the start of this exercise, it is clear from the above difference equation that

$$\frac{\partial q_t}{\partial q_{t-1}} = \frac{1-d_1}{1-d_1+d_2\rho\gamma} > 1.$$

Thus, the stochastic process for q_t is explosive, if central bank policy causes $r'_t = 0$ to hold each period.

Exercise 8.7

Suppose the central bank attempts to control the nominal money stock, rather than the nominal interest rate. Assume they target the level $\bar{m}$, which is consistent with the natural rate of output $\bar{y}$, and expected price level $\bar{p}$. Using the model given in Exercise 8.6, derive a stochastic difference equation for price level deviations from $\bar{p}$, which is driven by the stochastic shock terms and deviations in the money stock about $\bar{m}$. Determine a necessary condition as well as a sufficient condition for price level stability, assuming the central bank is able to eliminate systematic deviations of m_t from the target level.

Hint: Start by combining the first two model equations to eliminate r_t. Substitute $m_t = \overline{m}$, $p_t = \overline{p}$ and $y_t = \overline{y}$ into this equation. By definition, these values are simultaneously attained when each stochastic shock term equals zero (its unconditional expected value) and price level stability is anticipated.

Solution: $p'_t \equiv p_t - \overline{p}$ follows a second order stochastic difference equation.

$$p'_t = \phi_1 p'_{t-1} + \phi_2 p'_{t-2} - \frac{\gamma d_2 \left[m'_t - (1-\rho) m'_{t-1} \right]}{H - \gamma d_2 (1+\rho \alpha_2)} + \frac{v_t - (1-\rho) v_{t-1}}{H - \gamma d_2 (1+\rho \alpha_2)}$$

where:

$$\phi_1 \equiv \frac{2H - \gamma d_2 (1-\rho) - \alpha_2 d_2 \rho \gamma}{H - \gamma d_2 (1+\rho \alpha_2)},$$

$$\phi_2 \equiv \frac{-H}{H - \gamma d_2 (1+\rho \alpha_2)},$$

$v_t \equiv -\alpha_2 \gamma u_{1t} + d_2 \gamma u_{2t} + H u_{3t}$, and

$H \equiv -\alpha_2 (1 - d_1) - \alpha_1 d_2 > 0.$

Suppose the central bank pegs m_t, rendering the deviations $m'_t \equiv m_t - \overline{m}$ white noise (or setting $m'_t = 0\ \forall t$ if control is perfect). Then the following conditions are necessary for price level stability:

$\phi_2 > -1$, $\phi_2 < 1 - \phi_1$, and $\phi_2 < 1 + \phi_1$.

If these conditions are satisfied, the autoregressive coefficients lie within the so-called "stability triangle" of the parameter space. By utilizing these three conditions, and recalling the assumptions we made in Exercise 8.6 with respect to the underlying model parameters, we are able to demonstrate that

$1 + \rho \alpha_2 > 0$

is a necessary condition for stability. To ensure a stable process for p'_t, we must impose the more stringent sufficient condition

$2(1 + \alpha_2 \rho) - \rho > 0$.

9 The Representative Agent Model

Exercise 9.1

Consider a Ramsey economy, in which output is determined by the simple production function $Y(t) = F[K(t)]$, where $K(t)$ denotes the stock of capital and $Y(t)$ denotes the flow of output at time t. The supply of labor is fixed, and the production function exhibits positive but diminishing returns to capital. There is no depreciation.

Consider a central planner who wishes to maximize the utility of the representative agent:

$$W = \int_0^\infty U[C(t)] e^{-\beta t} dt,$$

where $U[\cdot]$ is an increasing, concave function of the flow of consumption, $C(t)$. Set up and solve the planner's problem, making sure to write out all optimality conditions, including the transversality condition. Derive and discuss the equations of motion for K and C as well as the steady state equilibrium conditions.

Hint: The rate of change of the capital stock is equal to savings at any time t.

Solution: Letting $\lambda(t)$ denote the costate variable corresponding to the state variable $K(t)$ (so that λ represents the marginal value of additional capital), the optimality conditions for the planner's problem are:

$$\lambda = U'(C),$$

$$\dot{\lambda} = \lambda\beta - \lambda F'(K),$$

$$\dot{K} = F(K) - C, \text{ and}$$

$$\lim_{t \to \infty} e^{-\beta t} \lambda(t) K(t) = 0.$$

The equations of motion for K and C are:

$$\dot{K} = F(K) - C, \text{ and}$$

$$\dot{C} = \frac{-U'(C)}{U''(C)}\left[F'(K) - \beta\right].$$

Setting $\dot{K} = \dot{C} = 0$, and recalling that $U'(C) > 0$ and $U''(C) < 0$, we derive the steady state equations:

$$C = F(K), \text{ and}$$

$$F'(K) = \beta.$$

Similar equations are interpreted in Section 9.2 of the text.

Exercise 9.2

Using the solution to Exercise 9.1, draw a phase diagram with K on the horizontal axis and C on the vertical axis. Does it make sense to talk about a "golden rule" level of the capital stock for this economy? Suppose there is a permanent decrease in the parameter β, meaning that the representative agent has become "more patient." Draw another phase diagram depicting the dynamic adjustment between the old and new equilibria. Will the economy end up with more or less capital?

Hint: Work very carefully through the dynamics for K and C away from the steady state point. Use this analysis to determine directional arrows for your phase diagram.

Solution: Your diagram should look something like the one shown below.

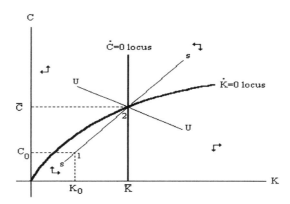

Beginning with initial capital stock K_0, the planner optimally chooses initial consumption C_0, resulting in a jump to point 1 on the stable arm SS. C and K adjust along SS over time, until we end up at point 2 in steady state.

There is no "golden rule" (i.e. steady state consumption-maximizing) level of the capital stock in this model. Graphically, this is reflected by the fact that the $\dot{K}=0$ locus has no maximum. This situation changes if we introduce exogenous population growth or a positive rate of capital depreciation.

We assumed that $F''(K)<0$. As a result, an increase in "patience" (i.e. lower β) must be accompanied by a rightward shift of the $\dot{C}=0$ locus, as depicted in the following phase diagram.

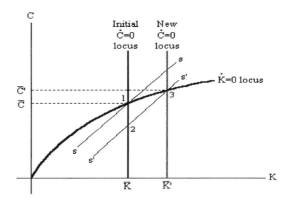

Assuming we are in steady state at point 1 prior to the decrease in β, the immediate effect is a drop in consumption. The economy then adjusts along

S'S' over time from point 2 to point 3, which is the new steady state. In the long run, we end up with a larger capital stock $(\overline{K}' > \overline{K})$ and more consumption $(\overline{C}' > \overline{C})$. The initial drop in consumption (i.e. increase in savings) makes possible an upward jump in investment $(I = F(K) - C)$, which begins the process of added capital accumulation.

Exercise 9.3

The graphical analysis of Exercise 9.2 can be done algebraically as well. First, compute the long run effect of a change in β on K and C. Second, linearize the equations of motion (from Exercise 9.1) and solve the resulting pair of differential equations. Use the transversality condition to rule out unstable paths, and assume $K(0) = K_0$ is exogenously given. Write down the solution with these boundary conditions imposed. Finally, derive an expression for the slope of the stable arm of the saddle path, which approximates the slope of S'S' near the steady state point in the phase diagram you used in Exercise 9.2. Show that this slope is positive and greater in magnitude than the long run partial derivative, thus confirming the transitional dynamics, as depicted in the phase diagram.

Hint: Before linearizing the equation of motion for $C(t)$, simplify notation by defining:

$$\sigma(C) = -\frac{U'(C)}{U''(C)}.$$

Solution: Let LR stand for long run (i.e. steady state) effects and SR stand for short run (i.e. transitional) effects. Over-bars are used to indicate steady state values of the endogenous variables. The long run effects of a change in β are:

$$\left.\frac{dK}{d\beta}\right|_{LR} = \frac{1}{F''(\overline{K})} < 0 \, ; \quad \left.\frac{dC}{d\beta}\right|_{LR} = \frac{F'(\overline{K})}{F''(\overline{K})} = \frac{\beta}{F''(\overline{K})} < 0 \, ; \quad \left.\frac{dC}{dK}\right|_{LR} = \beta > 0 \, .$$

The linearized system of differential equations describing the approximate time paths for $K(t)$ and $C(t)$ near the steady state is given below:

$$\begin{bmatrix} \dot{K} \\ \dot{C} \end{bmatrix} = \begin{bmatrix} \beta & -1 \\ F''(\overline{K}) \cdot \sigma(\overline{C}) & 0 \end{bmatrix} \begin{bmatrix} K - \overline{K} \\ C - \overline{C} \end{bmatrix}.$$

Let λ_1 and λ_2 be the characteristic roots of this system. We know that

$$\lambda_1 + \lambda_2 = \beta > 0 \text{ , and } \lambda_1 \lambda_2 = F''(\overline{K})\sigma(\overline{C}) < 0.$$

The second inequality implies that there is one negative root (say λ_1) and one positive root (say λ_2). In other words, the system is saddlepoint stable. The stable part of the solution to such a system is always associated with the negative root (λ_1). The general solution for the system is

$$\begin{bmatrix} K(t) \\ C(t) \end{bmatrix} = \begin{bmatrix} \overline{K} \\ \overline{C} \end{bmatrix} + c_1 \begin{bmatrix} 1 \\ \lambda_2 \end{bmatrix} e^{\lambda_1 t} + c_2 \begin{bmatrix} 1 \\ \lambda_1 \end{bmatrix} e^{\lambda_2 t},$$

where (lower-case) c_1 and c_2 are arbitrary constants. It can be shown that $c_2 = 0$ is necessary for satisfaction of the transversality condition. The initial condition then implies that $c_1 = K_0 - \overline{K}$, so we're left with the following stable solution:

$$\begin{bmatrix} K(t) \\ C(t) \end{bmatrix} = \begin{bmatrix} \overline{K} \\ \overline{C} \end{bmatrix} + (K_0 - \overline{K}) \begin{bmatrix} 1 \\ \lambda_2 \end{bmatrix} e^{\lambda_1 t} \xrightarrow[t \to \infty]{} \begin{bmatrix} \overline{K} \\ \overline{C} \end{bmatrix}.$$

The slope of the stable arm of the saddle path is given by

$$\left. \frac{dC}{dK} \right|_{SR} = \lambda_2 = \beta - \lambda_1 > \beta = \left. \frac{dC}{dK} \right|_{LR}.$$

Therefore, the second phase diagram in the solution to Exercise 9.2 is correctly drawn. The decrease in β is accompanied by an instantaneous *downward* jump in consumption, even though both C and K are greater in the long run, relative to the original equilibrium.

Exercise 9.4

A representative agent has production technology

$$Y(t) = F[K(t)] \; ; \; F'[K] > 0, F''[K] < 0.$$

Gross investment is given by

$$I(t) = \dot{K}(t) + \delta K(t),$$

where $0 < \delta < 1$ is the constant rate of depreciation. The agent chooses consumption, $C(t)$, each instant so as to maximize his discounted lifetime utility.

$$W = \int_0^\infty e^{-\beta t} U[C(t)] dt \quad ; \quad \beta > 0$$

The government collects lump sum taxes at rate τ, which it uses to finance expenditures at the constant rate G.

Solve the agent's problem, and use the optimality conditions to derive the equations of motion and steady state equations for $K(t)$ and $C(t)$. Use a phase diagram to analyze the effects of an increase in G, assuming the government balances its budget each instant. Does government spending crowd out private consumption, either partially or completely?

Hint: Output must be divided among consumption, investment and taxes. Use this market clearing condition to derive the agent's dynamic budget constraint.

Solution: The equations of motion are:

$$\dot{K} = F(K) - C - \tau - \delta K, \text{ and}$$

$$\dot{C} = -\frac{U'(C)}{U''(C)}[F'(K) - (\beta + \delta)].$$

The steady state equations result from setting $\dot{K} = \dot{C} = 0$, and the usual assumption that $U(C)$ is strictly increasing and strictly concave.

$$C = F(K) - \delta K - \tau$$

$$F'(K) = \beta + \delta$$

An increase in government expenditures is completely offset by a decrease in consumption, as shown in the phase diagram. Thus, there is 100% crowding out instantaneously. The capital stock is unaffected by the change in government expenditures.

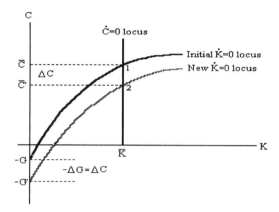

A downward jump immediately moves the economy from the old steady state (point 1) to the new steady state (point 2).

Exercise 9.5

Consider an economy in which output is produced according to a constant returns to scale technology, using capital (K) and government expenditures (G), which may represent a flow of production support services.

$$Y(t) = F[K(t), G(t)]$$

Assume that $F[\cdot]$ is strictly increasing and concave in both of its arguments. Capital does not depreciate. Suppose $G(t)$ is exogenously given, but a planner chooses consumption, $C(t)$, at each instant so as to maximize the following welfare function:

$$W = \int_0^\infty e^{-\beta t} U[C(t)] dt.$$

The felicity function, $U(C)$, is strictly increasing and concave. Write down the optimality conditions associated with the planner's problem. If the planner could choose G optimally, what additional optimality condition would this imply? Suppose we are initially in a steady state, where G happens to be set at its optimal (first best) level. Use a phase diagram to describe the dynamic adjustment of C and K in response to a small but permanent increase in G.

Hint: The assumptions made about the aggregate production function are sufficient to imply that $F_{KG} > 0$. Apply Euler's theorem to show this.

Solution: The optimality conditions are:

$$\lambda = U'(c),$$

$$\frac{\dot{\lambda}}{\lambda} = \beta - F_K(K,G),$$

$$\dot{K} = F(K,G) - C - G, \text{ and}$$

$$\lim_{t \to \infty} e^{-\beta t} \lambda(t) K(t) = 0,$$

where λ is the costate variable associated with the state variable, K. If G is chosen optimally, we add the condition $F_G(K,G) = 1$. This condition is approximately satisfied for a slight increase in G above its optimal level. In this case, the dynamic adjustment is depicted in the following phase diagram.

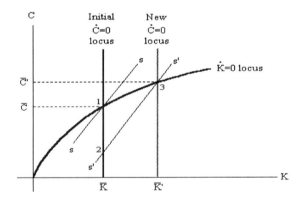

Consumption initially drops, moving the economy from point 1 to point 2. The economy then adjusts over time toward a new steady state at point 3. A more complete dynamic analysis is required to rigorously demonstrate that the initial jump in C must be downward, given the assumptions regarding the initial steady state $\left(F_G(\overline{K},G) = 1 \right)$.

Exercise 9.6

Suppose a central planner chooses consumption (C) and spending on a public good (G) each instant so as to maximize the representative agent's lifetime utility function.

$$W = \int_0^\infty e^{-\rho t}\{ln[C(t)]+\beta ln[G(t)]\}dt$$

The planner is constrained by the national income accounting identity

$$\dot{K}(t) = Y(t) - C(t) - G(t)$$

where K denotes the capital stock, and output is given by the following aggregate production function.

$$Y(t) = K(t)^\alpha$$

Derive the equations of motion and steady state expressions for K, C and G.

Hint: None.

Solution: The equations of motion are:

$$\dot{K} = K^\alpha - C - G,$$
$$\dot{C} = C[\alpha K^{\alpha-1} - \rho], \text{ and}$$
$$\dot{G} = \beta C[\alpha K^{\alpha-1} - \rho].$$

The optimal steady state values are given by the following expressions:

$$\overline{K} = \left[\frac{\rho}{\alpha}\right]^{\frac{1}{\alpha-1}} \quad \overline{C} = \frac{1}{1-\beta}\left[\frac{\rho}{\alpha}\right]^{\frac{\alpha}{\alpha-1}} \quad \overline{G} = \frac{\beta}{1+\beta}\left[\frac{\rho}{\alpha}\right]^{\frac{\alpha}{\alpha-1}}.$$

Exercise 9.7

A central planner chooses per capita consumption, $c(t) \equiv \dfrac{C(t)}{L(t)}$, so as to

$$\max \int_0^\infty e^{-\theta t} \frac{\sigma}{\sigma-1} c(t)^{\frac{\sigma-1}{\sigma}} dt, \quad \theta, \sigma > 0, \sigma \neq 1.$$

Aggregate output is produced according to a Cobb-Douglas technology,

$$Y(t) = K(t)^\alpha L(t)^{1-\alpha}, \quad 0 < \alpha < 1,$$

and the aggregate capital stock evolves according to the equation

$$\dot{K}(t) = I(t) - \delta K(t), \quad 0 < \delta < 1.$$

Goods market clearance requires that

$$Y(t) = C(t) + I(t)$$

each instant, and the initial capital stock is exogenously given as $K(0) = K_0$. Finally, the population grows at the constant rate n. This is also the rate of growth of the labor force $(i.e.\ \dot{L}/L \equiv n)$, since each individual is assumed to inelastically supply one unit of labor. Derive the expression for the rate of change of the capital-to-labor ratio, $\dot{k} \equiv \frac{d}{dt}[K(t)/L(t)]$, which constrains the planner's choices. Solve the planner's problem, deriving the equations of motion and steady state expressions for $k(t)$ and $c(t) \equiv C(t)/L(t)$. Derive an expression for the golden rule capital-to-labor ratio, and show that it exceeds the steady state capital-to-labor ratio.

Hint: None.

Solution: The capital-to-labor ratio evolves according to the following equation:

$$\dot{k}(t) = k(t)^\alpha - c(t) - (n+\delta)k(t).$$

The equations of motion are the preceding equation as well as an equation for $\dot{c}(t)$. Namely,

$$\dot{c}(t) = c(t) \cdot \sigma \left[\alpha k(t)^{\alpha-1} - (\theta + n + \delta) \right].$$

In steady state, we have

$$\bar{k} = \left[\frac{\theta + n + \delta}{\alpha} \right]^{\frac{1}{\alpha-1}}, \text{ and}$$

Chapter 9

$$\bar{c} = \bar{K}^\alpha - (n+\delta)\bar{k}.$$

The golden rule capital-to-labor ratio, which maximizes steady state per capita consumption, is given by the following expression.

$$k_{GR} = \left[\frac{n+\delta}{\alpha}\right]^{\frac{1}{\alpha-1}} > \bar{k}$$

Exercise 9.8

A central planner chooses per capita consumption, $c(t)$, so as to

$$\max \int_0^\infty e^{-\beta t} \ln[c(t)]dt \quad \beta > 0$$

s.t. $\dot{k}(t) = f[k(t)] - nk(t) - c(t),$

where the variables are defined as in Exercise 9.7. Suppose the economy is at the long run equilibrium point $(\bar{k}_1, \bar{c}_1)$ at time $t = 0$, when the planner learns that the population growth rate, n, will temporarily decrease from time $t = 0$ until time $t = T > 0$, at which time it returns to its previous level. Derive a set of equations describing (to a linear approximation) the optimal time paths of $k(t)$ and $c(t)$ during the time periods $0 \le t \le T$ and $t \ge T$.

Hint: The Appendix to Chapter 9 explains the basic method for solving this type of problem. Use a phase diagram to be sure you understand the long run and short run dynamics of this system, and how these dynamics are affected by a change in the variable n.

Solution: Letting $\mu_1 < 0$ represent the stable root of the system, $\mu_2 > 0$ represent the unstable root, and denoting the steady state associated with the temporary (lower) population growth rate by the ordered pair $(\bar{k}_2, \bar{c}_2)$, the dynamics of per capita consumption and the capital-to-labor ratio are completely described by the four equations shown below. Note that the characteristic roots of the system are not a function of n.

$0 \le t \le T$:

$$c(t) = \bar{c}_2 - (\bar{k}_2 - \bar{k}_1)\mu_2 e^{\mu_1 t}$$
$$+ e^{-\mu_2 T} \frac{\mu_1 e^{\mu_2 t} - \mu_2 e^{\mu_1 t}}{\mu_2 - \mu_1}\left[(\bar{c}_2 - \bar{c}_1) - \mu_2(\bar{k}_2 - \bar{k}_1)\right]$$

$$k(t) = \bar{k}_2 - (\bar{k}_2 - \bar{k}_1)e^{\mu_1 t} + e^{-\mu_2 T} \frac{e^{\mu_2 t} - e^{\mu_1 t}}{\mu_2 - \mu_1}\left[(\bar{c}_2 - \bar{c}_1) - \mu_2(\bar{k}_2 - \bar{k}_1)\right]$$

$t \geq T$:

$$c(t) = \bar{c}_1 - (\bar{k}_2 - \bar{k}_1)\mu_2 e^{\mu_1 t} + \frac{\mu_2 e^{\mu_1 t}}{\mu_2 - \mu_1}[\Omega]$$

$$k(t) = \bar{k}_1 - (\bar{k}_2 - \bar{k}_1)e^{\mu_1 t} + \frac{e^{\mu_1 t}}{\mu_2 - \mu_1}[\Omega]$$

$$\Omega \equiv \left(e^{-\mu_1 T} - e^{-\mu_2 T}\right)(\bar{c}_2 - \bar{c}_1) - \left(\mu_1 e^{-\mu_1 T} - \mu_2 e^{-\mu_2 T}\right)(\bar{k}_2 - \bar{k}_1)$$

10 Equilibrium in a Decentralized Economy with Distortionary Taxes and Inflation

Exercise 10.1

Consider a decentralized economy with households and firms. Households choose consumption, $C(t)$, and labor supply, $L(t)$, so as to

$$\max \int_0^\infty U[C(t), L(t)] e^{-\beta t} dt$$

s.t. $\dot{K}(t) = rK(t) + wL(t) - C(t); \quad K(0) = K_0,$

where K denotes physical capital (and also total wealth, since capital is the only asset), r is the fixed rate of return on capital and w is the fixed wage rate. There is no population growth, and we can normalize the number of households to equal one. Firms choose the amount of capital to rent and labor to hire from households each instant so as to maximize the net present value of profits over an infinite horizon.

$$\max \quad V = \int_0^\infty \{F[K(t), L(t)] - rK(t) - wL(t)\} e^{-\theta t} dt$$

Normalize the number of firms to equal one, and assume a constant returns to scale technology. Note that output is the numeraire commodity in this model.

Derive the optimality conditions for the representative household and firm as well as the associated steady state equations. Combine the latter equations to derive general equilibrium conditions defining the relationships among C, K and L in steady state.

Hint: Due to the existence of frictionless rental markets for its production inputs, the firm's problem is not truly a dynamic one. That is, it reduces to the static problem of maximizing profits each instant.

Solution: The current value Hamiltonian for the households is

$$H^* = U(C,L) + \lambda[rK + wL - C],$$

and the consumer's optimality conditions are:

$$U_C(C,L) - \lambda = 0,$$

$$U_L(C,L) + w\lambda = 0,$$

$$\dot{K} = rK + wL - C,$$

$$\dot{\lambda} = \lambda(\beta - r), \text{ and}$$

$$\lim_{t \to \infty} e^{-\beta t}\lambda(t)K(t) = 0.$$

The firm's optimality conditions are

$$w = F_L(K,L) \quad and \quad r = F_K(K,L).$$

Long run equilibrium is defined by the following steady state equations:

$$\overline{C} = F_K(\overline{K}, \overline{L}) \cdot \overline{K} + F_L(\overline{K}, \overline{L}) \cdot \overline{L}, \text{ and}$$

$$F_K(\overline{K}, \overline{L}) = \beta.$$

Exercise 10.2

Set up and solve the optimization problem for the centralized version of the economy described in Exercise 10.1, by assuming that the representative household has direct control over the production technology. Demonstrate that the same steady state equations result in the centralized model as in the decentralized model.

Hint: Utilize the homogeneity of the production function.

Solution: The representative agent's optimality conditions are as follows:

$$U_C(C,L) - \lambda = 0,$$

$$U_L(C,L) + \lambda F_L(K,L) = 0,$$

$$\dot{K} = F(K,L) - C,$$

$\dot{\lambda} = \lambda[\beta - F_K(K,L)]$, and

$\lim_{t \to \infty} e^{-\beta t} \lambda(t) K(t) = 0$.

Steady state is defined by the following equations, which are identical to those derived from the decentralized economy model given in Exercise 10.1.

$F_K(\overline{K}, \overline{L}) = \beta$

$\overline{C} = F(\overline{K}, \overline{L}) = F_K(\overline{K}, \overline{L}) \cdot \overline{K} + F_L(\overline{K}, \overline{L}) \cdot \overline{L}$

Note: Be careful not to confuse the costate variables from the centralized and decentralized problems. They are equivalent in this example, so I use the same symbol (λ) in both problems. In general, they will not be equivalent, and you should use two different symbols to avoid confusion.

Exercise 10.3

Add a government sector to the model given in Exercise 10.1. The household's total wealth, $A(t)$, is now composed of physical capital, $K(t)$, and government debt, $B(t)$. Physical capital pays rate of return r, as before, while government bonds pay the rate of interest i. The dynamic budget constraints faced by households and the government, respectively, are

$\dot{A}(t) \equiv \dot{K}(t) + \dot{B}(t) = rK(t) + iB(t) + wL(t) - C(t) - T(t)$, and

$\dot{B}(t) = iB(t) + G(t) - T(t)$,

where $G(t)$ is the flow rate of government expenditures and $T(t)$ is the flow of lump-sum taxes. Assume that initial asset stocks (K_0, B_0) are exogenously given. Derive the intertemporal budget constraints faced by households and the government, and show that Ricardian equivalence holds in this model.

Hint: The representative firm's optimality conditions are the same as in Exercise 10.1. Don't bother to substitute these expressions for r and w, since this would only complicate the resulting expressions. Of course, if the firm's problem were truly dynamic, we could not 'set aside' its optimality conditions in this fashion (see the Chapter 11 exercises).

Solution: The intertemporal budget constraints are shown below.

Households: $A_0 + \int_0^\infty e^{-rt} wL(t)dt = \int_0^\infty e^{-rt}\left[C(t) + T(t)\right]dt$

Government: $B_0 + \int_0^\infty e^{-rt} G(t)dt = \int_0^\infty e^{-rt} T(t)dt$

Combine the intertemporal budget constraints and derive the following equation:

$$K_0 + \int_0^\infty e^{-rt} wL(t)dt = \int_0^\infty e^{-rt}\left[C(t) + G(t)\right]dt.$$

Note that this last equation depends on neither taxes, $T(t)$, nor government debt, $B(t)$. Thus, Ricardian equivalence does hold in this model, since household decisions are unaffected by the timing of government debt and taxes, holding the path of government expenditures fixed. Equivalently, we can conclude that government bonds do not represent net wealth in this economy.

Exercise 10.4

Rework Exercise 10.3, but this time assume that taxes are levied on capital income: $T(t) = \tau r K(t)$. Assume the tax rate, τ, remains constant. Derive the intertemporal budget constraints for the consumer and the government, and show that Ricardian equivalence fails to hold in this case.

Hint: One of the consumer's optimality conditions, which is central to this problem, is a no-arbitrage relationship between the rates of return on private capital and government bonds.

Solution: The intertemporal budget constraints for the representative household and the government, respectively, are

$$A_0 + \int_0^\infty e^{-(1-\tau)rt} wL(t)dt = \int_0^\infty e^{-(1-\tau)rt} C(t)dt$$

$$B_0 + \int_0^\infty e^{-(1-\tau)rt} G(t)dt = \int_0^\infty e^{-(1-\tau)rt} \tau r K(t)dt$$

When we combine these two equations, using the identity $A_0 \equiv K_0 + B_0$, we find the following result.

$$K_0 + \int_0^\infty e^{-(1-\tau)rt} wL(t)dt = \int_0^\infty e^{-(1-\tau)rt} \left[C(t) + G(t) - \tau r K(t)\right]dt$$

The tax rate, τ, does not fall out, implying that Ricardian equivalence fails to hold in this model.

Exercise 10.5

In his 1967 article, "Rational Choice and Patterns of Growth in a Monetary Economy" (*American Economic Review*, 57, 534-544), Sidrauski develops a monetary growth model consisting of utility maximizing households, profit maximizing firms and a government that creates fiat money and rebates its seignorage revenue to consumers in lump sum fashion. Consider a simplified version of his model, with no population growth. Specifically, assume that consumers choose consumption (C), capital holdings (K), and real money holdings ($m \equiv M/P$) so as to:

max $\int_0^\infty U[C(t), m(t)] e^{-\beta t} dt$

s.t. $C(t) + \dot{K}(t) + \dot{m}(t) = w + rK(t) - \pi m(t) + X(t)$,

where

$\pi(t) \equiv \dfrac{\dot{P}(t)}{P(t)} \equiv$ the rate of inflation, and

$X(t) \equiv$ lump sum government transfers.

The constraint presumes that each consumer inelastically supplies one unit of labor per instant of time in return for wage income w and earns rental rate r per unit of capital provided to firms. Derive the consumer's optimality conditions.

Hint: None.

Solution: Letting λ denote the marginal value of wealth and β denote the consumer's rate of time preference, we have the following optimality conditions for the consumer's problem:

$U_C(C, m) = \lambda$,

$U_m(C,m) = (r+\pi)\lambda$,

$\dot{\lambda} = \lambda(\beta - r)$,

$\dot{m} + \dot{K} = w + rK - \pi m + X - C$, and

$\lim_{t \to \infty} e^{-\beta t}\lambda(t)m(t) = \lim_{t \to \infty} e^{-\beta t}\lambda(t)K(t) = 0$.

Exercise 10.6

Sidrauski's model is closed by imposing the firm's optimality conditions and the government budget constraint:

$r = F'(K)$, $w = F(K) - KF'(K)$, and $X = \sigma m$, where

$\sigma \equiv \dfrac{\dot{M}}{M} \equiv$ the fixed rate of growth of the nominal money supply.

Combine these conditions with the consumer optimality conditions derived in Exercise 10.5 and show that money is superneutral in the long run.

Hint: None.

Solution: The general equilibrium equations of motion are:

$\dot{K} = F(K) - C$,

$\dot{\lambda} = \lambda[\beta - F'(K)]$, and

$\dot{m} = m(\sigma - \pi)$.

By setting $\dot{K} = \dot{\lambda} = \dot{m} = 0$, we derive the following steady state equations:

$F(K) - C = 0$,

$\beta - F'(K) = 0$, and

$\sigma - \pi = 0$.

The real variables (C, K) are determined by the first two steady state equations independently of the rate of nominal money growth, σ. This implies that, outside of transitional adjustments, money is superneutral in this model.

In the long run, there is a one-to-one relationship between the rate of nominal money growth and the rate of inflation.

Exercise 10.7

Is money superneutral, both in transition and in the long run, if consumer preferences take the Cobb-Douglas form shown below?

$$U(C,m) = C^\theta m^{1-\theta}, \quad 0 < \theta < 1$$

What if preferences take the following logarithmic form?

$$U(C,m) = \ln(C) + \theta \ln(m)$$

Explain why these two cases differ, and derive the static relationship between consumption and the money stock. Also, derive a dynamic equation relating the proportional rates of change of m and C and the rate of change of K, assuming preferences take the Cobb-Douglas form specified above.

Hint: Use the consumer's static optimality conditions.

Solution: The explanations are provided in the text. The following static relationship between C and m clearly demonstrates that, when preferences are Cobb Douglas, money is *not* superneutral in the short run.

$$C = \frac{\theta}{1-\theta}[F'(K) + \pi]m \quad \Rightarrow \quad \left.\frac{dC}{dm}\right|_{SR} > 0 \quad \text{if} \quad \pi > -F'(K)$$

Taking time derivatives of the static optimality conditions and combining the results so as to eliminate the costate variable, λ, and its time derivative, we arrive at the following dynamic equation:

$$\frac{\dot{C}}{C} = \frac{\dot{m}}{m} + \frac{F''(K)}{F'(K) + \pi}\dot{K}.$$

11 A Dynamic Analysis of Taxes

Exercise 11.1

Consider a version of the model outlined in Chapter 11 with the following simplifications:

- There are no investment adjustment costs.

- The dividend yield $(i \equiv D/sE)$ is exogenously set at some constant between zero and one, effectively fixing the firm's financial structure.

- Total wealth, A, is equal to the value of government bonds, B, plus the value of corporate equities, sE. Define the wealth share of bonds as $\phi \equiv B/A$ and the wealth share of corporate equities as $1 - \phi \equiv sE/A$.

Set up and solve the consumer's infinite horizon utility maximization problem, assuming the existence of an interior optimum with $C > 0$, $L > 0$ and $0 < \phi < 1$.

Hint: . The control variables are C, L and ϕ, while the state variable is A. Also, remember to apply the product rule when computing $\dot{A}$.

Solution: The consumer seeks to

$$\max_{C, L, \phi} \int_0^\infty U(C, L) e^{-\beta t} dt \quad , \quad 0 < \beta < 1$$

s.t. $\quad \dot{A} = (1 - \tau_Y)\left[wL + r\phi A + i(1 - \phi)A\right] + (1 - \tau_c)\frac{\dot{s}}{s}(1 - \phi)A - C$.

The current value Hamiltonian for this problem is

$$H^* = U(C, L) + \lambda \left\{ (1 - \tau_Y)\left[wL + r\phi A + i(1 - \phi)A\right] + (1 - \tau_c)\frac{\dot{s}}{s}(1 - \phi)A - C \right\},$$

giving rise to the following optimality conditions:

$$\lambda = U_c(C,L),$$

$$(1-\tau_y)w = -\frac{U_L(C,L)}{U_c(C,L)},$$

$$(1-\tau_y)r = (1-\tau_y)i + (1-\tau_c)\frac{\dot{s}}{s},$$

$$\dot{A} = (1-\tau_y)\left[wL + r\phi A + i(1-\phi)A\right] + (1-\tau_c)\frac{\dot{s}}{s}(1-\phi)A - C,$$

$$\frac{\dot{\lambda}}{\lambda} = \beta - \phi(1-\tau_y)r - (1-\phi)\left[(1-\tau_y)i + (1-\tau_c)\frac{\dot{s}}{s}\right], \text{ and}$$

$$\lim_{t\to\infty} e^{-\beta t}\lambda A = 0.$$

Exercise 11.2

Continuing with the simplified model set out in Exercise 11.1, set up and solve the firm's infinite horizon value maximization problem. Derive an expression for the firm's cost of capital, which explicitly incorporates the consumer's optimality conditions.

Hint: Do not confuse $\theta \equiv \beta - \dot{\lambda}/\lambda$, *which represents the rate of return on consumption, with the firm's cost of capital,* θ^*. *Also, recall the assumption that* $i \equiv D/sE$ *is exogenously fixed at a value between zero and one.*

Solution: The firm chooses L and K so as to

$$\max \; V(0) = \int_0^\infty e^{-\int_0^t \theta^*(\tau)d\tau} \left\{(1-\tau_p)\left[F(K,L) - wL\right] - \dot{K}\right\}dt.$$

The firm raises only equity capital, and the cost of that capital is given directly by the following expression.

$$\theta^*(\tau) = i(\tau) + \frac{\dot{s}(\tau)}{s(\tau)}$$

Letting $\theta \equiv \beta - \dot{\lambda}/\lambda$ and incorporating two optimality conditions from the solution to Exercise 11.1, we can write the expression for the firm's cost of capital as

$$\theta^* = \theta + \frac{\theta \tau_C + i(\tau_Y - \tau_C)}{1 - \tau_C}.$$

This expression demonstrates how the consumer "drives" the firm's cost of capital, since θ is a function of the consumer's preferences and decisions.

We can solve the firm's value maximization problem by the calculus of variations method. The resulting optimality conditions simultaneously determine the firm's demand for labor and capital:

$$F_L(K, L) = w, \text{ and}$$

$$(1 - \tau_P) F_K(K, L) = \theta^* = i + \frac{\dot{s}}{s}.$$

Note the static nature of these optimality conditions.

Exercise 11.3

We can combine the consumer optimality conditions from Exercise 11.1, the firm optimality conditions from Exercise 11.2, and the market clearing condition

$$\dot{K} = F(K, L) - C - G,$$

to form a complete general equilibrium dynamic system. I'm relying on the fact, as shown in Chapter 10, that Tobin's q is always equal to 1 in this model. Thus, $V(t) = K(t) \,\forall t$.

The first two consumer optimality conditions and the first firm optimality condition can be solved simultaneously for the choice functions $C = C(K, \lambda)$ and $L = L(K, \lambda)$. Although C and L would also depend on the tax rate, τ_Y, we suppress this argument for convenience. Derive expressions for the short run partial derivatives: C_K, C_λ, L_K and L_λ. Determine the signs of these expressions, assuming that both the utility and production functions are strictly concave and that consumption and leisure are complementary goods.

Combine the Exercise 11.2 expressions for the firm's cost of capital, θ^*, to derive a static expression for the rate of return on consumption, θ. Substitute the labor supply function, $L(K, \lambda)$, into this expression to derive the short run function, $\theta(K, \lambda)$, and then sign the partial derivatives θ_K and θ_λ.

The equations of motion for λ and K are

$\dot{\lambda} = \lambda[\beta - \theta(K,\lambda)]$, and

$\dot{K} = F[K, L(K,\lambda)] - C(K,\lambda) - G$.

Using the short run choice functions, which you just derived, try to sign the slopes of the steady state loci in (K,λ) space.

Hint: You can ignore the government budget constraint, which must be satisfied by Walras' law.

Solution: Define $\Delta \equiv (U_{CC} U_{LL} - U_{CL}^2) + U_{CC}\lambda(1-\tau_Y) F_{LL} > 0$. Show that:

$$C_K \equiv \left.\frac{dC}{dK}\right|_{SR} = \frac{1}{\Delta}\left[\lambda(1-\tau_Y) F_{LK} U_{CL}\right] < 0,$$

$$C_\lambda \equiv \left.\frac{dC}{d\lambda}\right|_{SR} = \frac{1}{\Delta}\left[U_{LL} + U_{CL}(1-\tau_Y) F_L + \lambda(1-\tau_Y) F_{LL}\right] < 0,$$

$$L_K \equiv \left.\frac{dL}{dK}\right|_{SR} = \frac{1}{\Delta}\left[-\lambda(1-\tau_Y) F_{LK} U_{CC}\right] > 0, \text{ and}$$

$$L_\lambda \equiv \left.\frac{dL}{d\lambda}\right|_{SR} = \frac{1}{\Delta}\left[-(1-\tau_Y) F_L U_{CC} - U_{CL}\right] > 0.$$

The short run function $\theta = \theta(K,\lambda)$ is given by

$$\theta = (1-\tau_C)(1-\tau_P) F_K[K, L(K,\lambda)] - i(\tau_Y - \tau_C),$$

and its first derivatives are given by the following expressions:

$$\theta_K \equiv \left.\frac{d\theta}{dK}\right|_{SR} = (1-\tau_C)(1-\tau_P)[F_{KK} + F_{KL} L_K] < 0, \text{ and}$$

$$\theta_\lambda \equiv \left.\frac{d\theta}{d\lambda}\right|_{SR} = (1-\tau_C)(1-\tau_P) F_{KL} L_\lambda > 0.$$

Finally, the slopes of the steady state loci near the point of long run equilibrium are given by the following partial derivatives:

$$\left.\frac{d\lambda}{dK}\right|_{\dot\lambda=0} = -\frac{F_{KK} + F_{KL} L_K}{F_{KL} L_\lambda} > 0, \text{ and}$$

$$\left.\frac{d\lambda}{dK}\right|_{\dot{K}=0} = -\frac{F_K + F_L L_K + C_K}{F_L L_\lambda - C_\lambda} \gtrless 0.$$

Stability conditions may require some restriction on the sign of the $\dot{K} = 0$ locus. In order to determine whether this is the case, you would proceed by writing down the linearized dynamic system for K and λ.

Exercise 11.4

Consider an economy with a representative consumer and a representative firm. There is no government in this economy, and therefore no taxes. The consumer allocates his income each instant between consumption and savings, with the latter invested in shares of equity in the representative firm. There is only one consumption good, which is numeraire, and a share of equity sells for relative price $s(t)$ at time t. The consumer, who is assumed to possess a logarithmic felicity function, maximizes lifetime utility over an infinite horizon, subject to the appropriate dynamic budget constraint.

The representative firm produces goods, using only capital, according to the following technology:

$$Y(t) = F[K(t)] = 2K(t)^{\frac{1}{2}}.$$

There is no depreciation, so the firm's capital stock evolves according to the equation $K(t) = I(t)$, where $I(t)$ represents gross investment. The numeraire consumption good may be retained as capital, but there is an adjustment cost to install capital. Assume this adjustment cost takes the form $\psi(I) = (1/2)I^2$. The firm, which does not issue any debt instruments, is exogenously constrained to pay a fixed dividend yield, i. Any remaining cash flow is invested in new capital.

Set up and solve both the consumer's and the firm's dynamic optimization problems. Derive an expression for the firm's cost of capital, $\theta = \theta(K, q)$, which depends upon the consumer's preferences and is consistent with goods market clearance. The variable q represents the marginal value of capital to the firm.

Hint: Goods market clearance requires that $Y(t) = C(t) + I(t)$.

Solution: The representative consumer seeks to

$$\max_{C(t)} \int_0^\infty e^{-\beta t} \ln[C(t)] dt$$

s.t. $s(t)\dot{E}(t) + C(t) = is(t)E(t)$.

The consumer's optimality conditions are:

$s = C\lambda$,

$s\dot{E} + C = isE$,

$\dot{C} = C(\theta - \beta)$, and

$$\lim_{t\to\infty} e^{-\beta t} \frac{sE}{C} = 0$$

where $\theta \equiv i + \dot{s}/s \equiv$ the firm's cost of capital, and λ is the marginal value of wealth.

The representative firm seeks to

$$\max_{I(t)} \int_0^\infty e^{-\int_0^t \theta(\tau)d\tau} \left[2K(t)^{\frac{1}{2}} - I(t) - \frac{1}{2}I(t)^2 \right] dt$$

s.t. $\dot{K}(t) = I(t)$,

giving rise to the following optimality conditions:

$q = 1 + I$,

$\dot{K} = I = q - 1$,

$\dot{q} = \theta q - K^{-\frac{1}{2}}$, and

$$\lim_{t\to\infty} e^{-\int_0^t \theta(\tau)d\tau} qK = 0.$$

The firm's cost of capital is given by

$$\theta = \theta(K, q) = \beta + \frac{K^{-\frac{1}{2}} - \beta}{2K^{\frac{1}{2}} + 1} q.$$

Exercise 11.5

Suppose the economy described in Exercise 11.4 is in steady state, with $\dot{C} = \dot{K} = \dot{q} = 0$ (see the hint given below). Derive the steady state levels of q, K and C, using the equations of motion, the market clearing equation, and the function $\theta = \theta(K,q)$ you found in the previous exercise. Take a linear approximation to the equations of motion for q and K (but not C) about the steady state and draw a phase diagram for this linearized system.

Hint: The equations of motion for C, q and K are recursive, allowing us to study the dynamics of q and K separately. A complete steady state in λ, s and E (as well as C, q and K) is possible only if $i = \beta$. Assume this condition is satisfied. It can then be shown that the steady state value of the firm is equal to the capitalized value of all future output:

$$\bar{s} \cdot \bar{E} = \frac{Y}{\beta}.$$

Solution: The steady state levels of q, K and C are shown below.

$$\bar{q} = 1 \quad , \quad \bar{K} = \frac{1}{\beta^2} \quad , \quad \bar{C} = \frac{2}{\beta}$$

The linearized dynamic system for q and K is

$$\begin{bmatrix} \dot{q} \\ \dot{K} \end{bmatrix} = \begin{bmatrix} \beta & \frac{\beta^3}{\beta+2} \\ 1 & 0 \end{bmatrix} \begin{bmatrix} q-1 \\ K - \frac{1}{\beta^2} \end{bmatrix},$$

where all derivatives appearing in the coefficient matrix have been evaluated at the steady state. The phase diagram is shown below. Beginning from the initial capital stock, K_0, it is optimal to jump onto the stable arm of the saddle path (SS) and proceed along this path to the steady state point:

$$(\bar{K}, \bar{q}) = \left(1/\beta^2, 1\right).$$

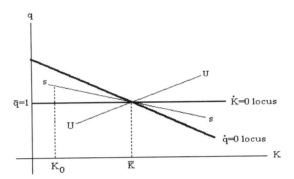

Exercise 11.6

Solve the linearized dynamic system for $q(t)$ and $K(t)$ you derived in Exercise 11.5. Show that a sufficient condition for the firm's transversality condition to be satisfied is that the coefficient on the unstable portion of the general solution be constrained to equal zero. Use the initial condition $K(0) = K_0$ to solve for the other constant and write down the solution that satisfies both boundary conditions. Demonstrate algebraically that the stable arm of the saddle path slopes downward, but not as steeply as the $\dot{q} = 0$ locus (as depicted in the phase diagram).

Hint: None.

Solution: The general solution is

$$\begin{bmatrix} q(t) \\ K(t) \end{bmatrix} = \begin{bmatrix} 1 \\ 1/\beta^2 \end{bmatrix} + a_1 \begin{bmatrix} z_1 \\ 1 \end{bmatrix} e^{\mu_1 t} + a_2 \begin{bmatrix} z_2 \\ 1 \end{bmatrix} e^{\mu_2 t},$$

where a_1 and a_2 are arbitrary constants and μ_1 and μ_2 are the eigenvalues of the system, with corresponding eigenvectors $[z_1 \ 1]$ and $[z_2 \ 1]$. The eigenvalues satisfy the characteristic equation

$$\mu_i^2 - \beta\mu_i - \frac{\beta^3}{\beta+2} = 0, \quad (i = 1, 2),$$

while the eigenvectors satisfy the following system by definition.

$$\begin{bmatrix} \beta-\mu_i & \dfrac{\beta^3}{\beta+2} \\ 1 & -\mu_i \end{bmatrix} \begin{bmatrix} z_i \\ 1 \end{bmatrix} = \begin{bmatrix} 0 \\ 0 \end{bmatrix}, \quad (i=1,2)$$

The lower equation implies that $z_i = \mu_i$ for $i=1,2$. The solution satisfying both boundary conditions is:

$$\begin{bmatrix} q(t) \\ K(t) \end{bmatrix} = \begin{bmatrix} 1 \\ 1/\beta^2 \end{bmatrix} + \left(K_0 - (1/\beta^2)\right)\begin{bmatrix} \mu_1 \\ 1 \end{bmatrix} e^{\mu_1 t} \xrightarrow[t\to\infty]{} \begin{bmatrix} 1 \\ 1/\beta^2 \end{bmatrix} = \begin{bmatrix} \overline{q} \\ \overline{K} \end{bmatrix},$$

where μ_1 is the stable (negative) root. It is straightforward to show that

$$(q-1) = \mu_1\left(K - (1/\beta^2)\right),$$

so that the slope of the stable arm is negative.

$$\left.\dfrac{dq}{dK}\right|_{ss} = \mu_1 < 0$$

We know from the coefficient matrix of the linearized system that

$\mu_1 + \mu_2 = \beta > 0$, and

$$\mu_1 \cdot \mu_2 = \beta \cdot \dfrac{-\beta^2}{\beta+2} = \beta \cdot \left(\left.\dfrac{dq}{dK}\right|_{\dot{q}=0}\right) < 0.$$

Given our assumption that μ_1 is the stable root, the unstable root is given by $\mu_2 = \beta - \mu_1 > \beta$. Since

$$\left.\dfrac{dq}{dK}\right|_{ss} = \dfrac{\beta}{\mu_2}\left(\left.\dfrac{dq}{dK}\right|_{\dot{q}=0}\right) < 0, \text{ and } 0 < \dfrac{\beta}{\mu_2} < 1,$$

we conclude that the stable arm of the saddle path is downward-sloping, but not so steeply downward-sloping as the $\dot{q} = 0$ locus. This confirms that the phase diagram was drawn correctly in the previous exercise.

Exercise 11.7

In his book, *The Investment Decisions of Firms* (1978, Cambridge University Press), S. J. Nickell presents a partial equilibrium model of investment for a monopolist. We can simplify the model by assuming some convenient functional forms. The firm faces a downward-sloping demand for its output:

$$Y(t)^D = \beta(t)P(t)^\alpha \quad , \beta(t) > 0 \, \forall \, t \quad \text{and} \quad \alpha < -1.$$

$\beta(t)$ is a time-varying demand shift parameter, while α is the constant price elasticity of demand. The firm acquires labor (L) and capital (K) from perfectly competitive factor markets and uses the inputs to produce output with a Cobb-Douglas technology:

$$Y(t)^S = K(t)^\phi L(t)^{1-\phi} \quad , \quad 0 < \phi < 1.$$

Capital depreciates at the constant rate δ, so the equation of motion for capital is $\dot{K}(t) = I(t) - \delta K(t)$, where $I(t)$ represents the flow of gross investment.

The firm's objective is to maximize the present value of all future net cash flows over an infinite horizon, subject to the capital stock evolution constraint. We assume that the firm may borrow or lend as much as it wishes at a fixed rate, and that capital may be installed instantaneously without adjustment costs. Under these conditions, the firm's problem is really the static one of maximizing profits each instant.

Use the firm's optimality conditions (including the capital accumulation constraint) and the market clearing condition $(Y^S = Y^D = Y)$ to derive an expression for the investment-to-capital ratio (I/K) involving the rate of demand growth $(\dot{\beta}/\beta)$, the depreciation rate (δ) and the rate of change in wages $(\dot{w}/w)$ and the user cost of capital $(\dot{c}/c)$.

Hint: Profit maximization requires that $c = MRP_K = MR_Y MP_K$. Take advantage of the homogeneity of the production function to work in terms of output per unit of labor $(y \equiv Y/L)$ and the capital-to-labor ratio $(k \equiv K/L)$. Logarithmically differentiate the market clearing condition and the factor market tangency conditions.

Solution: $\dfrac{I}{K} = \dfrac{\dot{\beta}}{\beta} + \delta + (1+\alpha)(1-\phi)\dfrac{\dot{w}}{w} - (1-\phi-\alpha\phi)\dfrac{\dot{c}}{c}$

12 The Representative Agent in the International Economy

Exercise 12.1

Consider the following discrete time model of a small open economy, which is presented by Maurice Obstfeld and Kenneth Rogoff in their forthcoming book entitled *Foundations of International Macroeconomics*. A representative agent chooses consumption and investment in each period so as to maximize lifetime utility over an infinite horizon, subject to certain constraints.

$$\max \sum_{t=0}^{\infty} \beta^t u(C_t) \qquad u' > 0, u'' < 0$$

s.t. $\quad B_t = Y_t - G_t + (1+r)B_{t-1} - C_t - I_t$

$\qquad Y_t = A_t F(K_{t-1}) \quad F' > 0, F'' < 0, A_t > 0$

$\qquad I_t = K_t - K_{t-1}$

The variables in the model are defined as follows:

- $\beta \equiv$ the representative agent's subjective discount factor,
- $C_t \equiv$ consumption during period t,
- $B_t \equiv$ stock of foreign bonds held at time t,
- $r \equiv$ constant world interest rate,
- $Y_t \equiv$ output during period t,
- $G_t \equiv$ government expenditures during period t,
- $I_t \equiv$ investment during period t,
- $K_t \equiv$ capital stock at time t, and
- $A_t \equiv$ exogenous productivity parameter for time t.

The agent's prior consumption choices impact the state variables B_t and K_t, while A_t, G_t and r are exogenous state variables.

Set up and solve the representative agent's optimization problem.

Hint: A condition is required to rule out ponzi schemes, whereby the agent acquires debt $(B_t < 0)$ at a rate that exceeds the world interest rate.

Solution: There are several methods for solving this problem, including Lagrangean techniques and direct substitution. The method of dynamic programming is convenient here, because it takes advantage of the recursive structure of the problem. Denote the value function at time t by $V(B_t, K_t; \cdot)$, so as to emphasize the state variables that are impacted by the agent's choices. The Bellman equation is

$$V(B_{t-1}, K_{t-1}; \cdot) = \max_{C_t, I_t} \left[u(C_t) + \beta V(B_t, K_t; \cdot) \right]$$

s.t. $B_t = A_t F(K_{t-1}) - G_t + (1+r)B_{t-1} - C_t - I_t$

$K_t = K_{t-1} + I_t$,

giving rise to two static optimality conditions and two envelope conditions. These four equations may be combined into a pair of Euler equations:

$u'(C_t) = \beta(1+r)u'(C_{t+1})$, and

$A_{t+1} F'(K_t) = r$.

Ponzi schemes are ruled out by the following condition:

$$\lim_{t \to \infty} \left(\frac{1}{1+r} \right)^t B_t = 0.$$

Exercise 12.2

Utilize the budget constraint and the No-Ponzi-Game (NPG) condition from Exercise 12.1 to derive the representative agent's lifetime budget constraint. Given this constraint, is it feasible for a country to run current account deficits $(B_t - B_{t-1} < 0)$ forever?

Hint: Starting from an initial stock of foreign bonds, B_0, perform recursive substitutions (forward in time) on the flow budget constraint. Impose the NPG condition.

Solution: The agent's lifetime budget constraint may be written in the following form:

$$-(1+r)B_0 = \sum_{t=1}^{\infty}\left(\frac{1}{1+r}\right)^{t-1} X_t$$

where $X_t \equiv Y_t - C_t - I_t - G_t$. Suppose $B_0 < 0$, meaning the country is in debt to the rest of the world at time $t = 0$. Then $-(1+r)B_0 > 0$, implying that positive net exports $(X_t > 0)$ will be required in some future time periods, if the lifetime budget constraint is to be satisfied. However, the current account is defined as the sum of net exports and interest payments on past debt.

$$CA_t \equiv B_t - B_{t-1} = rB_{t-1} + X_t$$

Clearly, it is possible for $X_t > 0$ and $CA_t < 0$ to hold at the same time, given that $rB_{t-1} < 0$ for a debtor country. Thus it is feasible for a country to run current account deficits forever, in the sense that such behavior does not necessarily violate that country's intertemporal budget constraint.

Exercise 12.3

Suppose it happens that $(1+r)\beta = 1$, so the factor by which the representative agent discounts future consumption just equals the discount factor implied by the world interest rate. Use the optimality conditions from Exercise 12.1 and the intertemporal budget constraint from Exercise 12.2 to analyze the qualitative effect on the current account of a temporary positive output shock. Determine the effect of a temporary government expenditure shock on the current account as well.

Hint: Given the assumption made at the start of this exercise, it is optimal to perfectly smooth consumption over time. This is evident from one of the Euler conditions derived in Exercise 12.1.

Solution: Starting from some arbitrary initial time period, we can write the intertemporal budget constraint as follows:

$$\sum_{s=t}^{\infty}\left(\frac{1}{1+r}\right)^{s-t}C_s = (1+r)B_{t-1} + \sum_{s=t}^{\infty}\left(\frac{1}{1+r}\right)^{s-t}[Y_s - I_s - G_s].$$

With $\beta(1+r) = 1$, the agent will want to consume the same amount in each period (i.e., set $C_t = C_{t+1} = \cdots$), since one of the Euler equations simplifies to

$$u'(C_t) = u'(C_{t+1}) \quad \forall t.$$

This allows us to pull C_t outside the infinite sum (in the intertemporal budget constraint given above) and solve for the consumption function,

$$C_t = rB_{t-1} + Y_t^P - I_t^P - G_t^P,$$

where:

$$Y_t^P \equiv \frac{r}{1+r}\sum_{s=t}^{\infty}\left(\frac{1}{1+r}\right)^{s-t} Y_s \equiv \text{permanent income},$$

$$I_t^P \equiv \frac{r}{1+r}\sum_{s=t}^{\infty}\left(\frac{1}{1+r}\right)^{s-t} I_s \equiv \text{permanent investment, and}$$

$$G_t^P \equiv \frac{r}{1+r}\sum_{s=t}^{\infty}\left(\frac{1}{1+r}\right)^{s-t} G_s \equiv \text{permanent government expenditures}.$$

Substitute this form of the consumption function into the current account, as given by

$$CA_t = rB_{t-1} + Y_t - G_t - C_t - I_t,$$

and solve for the following equation:

$$CA_t = (Y_t - Y_t^P) - (G_t - G_t^P) - (I_t - I_t^P).$$

We can immediately see from this equation that temporary increases in national income increase the current account, while temporary increases in government expenditures reduce the current account.

Exercise 12.4

The following model, due to Partha Sen and Stephen Turnovsky (1989, *International Economic Review*, 30, 811-31), is very similar to the model presented in Section 12.3 of the text. The most important difference is the introduction of a tariff, allowing for a macrodynamic analysis of the effect of changes in the tariff rate. The government does not purchase any goods in this version of the model, as all tariff revenues are rebated to the representative consumer in lump sum fashion. The consumer chooses consumption of domestic goods (x) foreign goods (y) and labor supply (L) so as to

$$\max \int_0^\infty [U(x,y)+V(L)]e^{-\delta t}dt$$

s.t. $\dot{b} = \frac{1}{\sigma}[\pi + wL - x] - \gamma y + i^* b + T \quad ; \quad b(0) = b_0,$

where:

$\pi \equiv$ real profits received by the consumer,

$\gamma \equiv$ $1+\tau$, where τ is the tariff rate,

$w \equiv$ real wage in terms of domestic goods,

$T \equiv$ lump sum government transfers,

and all other notation matches Section 12.3 of the text.

The representative firm chooses labor input and investment so as to

$$\max \int_0^\infty \pi(t)e^{-R(t)}dt$$

s.t. $\dot{K} = I$ and $K(0) = K_0,$

where:

$\pi(t) \equiv F[K(t), L(t)] - wL(t) - C[I(t)],$

$R(t) \equiv \int_0^t i(s)ds,$

and all other notation follows Section 12.3 of the text. Recall that the domestic real interest rate, $i(t)$, is related to the foreign real interest rate, $i^*(t)$, by the uncovered interest rate parity condition:

$$i(t) = i^*(t) + \frac{\dot{\sigma}}{\sigma}.$$

The utility, production and investment cost functions possess all of the properties noted in the text. Finally, the government budget constraint is given by the equation:

$(\gamma - 1)y = T$.

Solve the household and firm optimization problems. Write out a set of equations that define the macroeconomic equilibrium in this decentralized economy, including a market clearing condition for domestic goods. Assume (as in Section 12.3 of the text) that $\delta = i^*$, thus ensuring the existence of a well-defined steady state.

Hint: The firm finances investment by retained earnings and takes $i(t)$ as exogenously give, while the representative household takes $\pi(t)$ as exogenous.

Solution: Given the assumption that $\delta = i^*$, the marginal utility of wealth is always equal to its steady state value, $\overline{\lambda}$. Macroeconomic equilibrium is characterized by the following equations:

$$U_x(x, y) = \frac{\overline{\lambda}}{\sigma},$$

$$U_y(x, y) = \overline{\lambda}\gamma,$$

$$V'(L) = -\frac{\overline{\lambda}}{\sigma} F_L(K, L),$$

$$C'(I) = q,$$

$$F(K, L) = x + Z(\sigma) + C(I) \quad ; \quad Z'(\sigma) > 0,$$

$$\dot{q} = \left(i^* + \frac{\dot{\sigma}}{\sigma}\right) q - F_K(K, L),$$

$$\dot{K} = I(q), \text{ and}$$

$$\dot{b} = \frac{1}{\sigma}[F(K, L) - C(I) - x] - y - i^* b.$$

$Z(\sigma)$ represents exports of the domestic good, which are assumed to be an increasing function of the real exchange rate. Finally, the transversality conditions for the household and the firm are

$$\lim_{t \to \infty} b(t) e^{-i^* t} = 0, \text{ and}$$

$$\lim_{t \to \infty} q(t) K(t) e^{-R(t)} = 0.$$

Exercise 12.5

It is clear from the macroeconomic system derived in Exercise 12.4, that one can solve the linearized differential equations for $q(t)$ and $K(t)$ first, and then determine $b(t)$ in a subsequent step. Thus, the core of this dynamic system, to a linear approximation near steady state, is given by the following pair of differential equations:

$$\begin{bmatrix} \dot{q}(t) \\ \dot{K}(t) \end{bmatrix} = \begin{bmatrix} \omega_{11} & \omega_{12} \\ 1/C''(\bar{I}) & 0 \end{bmatrix} \begin{bmatrix} q(t) - \bar{q} \\ K(t) - \bar{K} \end{bmatrix}.$$

This system is saddlepoint stable, since it turns out that $\omega_{12} > 0$. Derive the equations describing the paths of $q(t)$ and $K(t)$ along the stable arm of the saddle path, and demonstrate that the steady state stock of foreign bonds, $\bar{b}$, depends on the initial stocks of foreign bonds (b_0) and capital (K_0).

Hint: Utilize the market clearing condition for the domestic good to rewrite the accumulation equation for foreign bonds. Linearize this equation around steady state, making use of the functions, $\sigma = \sigma(\bar{\lambda}, k, q)$ and $y = y(\bar{\lambda}, K, q)$, which are implied by the static optimality conditions.

Solution: The dynamics of the capital stock and its shadow value along the stable arm of the saddle path are described by the following equations:

$$K(t) - \bar{K} = (K_0 - \bar{K})e^{\mu_1 t}, \text{ and}$$

$$q(t) - \bar{q} = \left[\frac{\mu_1}{I_q}\right][K(t) - \bar{K}],$$

where $\mu_1 < 0$ is the stable root of the system, and $I_q \equiv \partial I(q)/\partial q > 0$.

We can write the accumulation equation for foreign bonds in the form

$$\dot{b}(t) = \frac{Z[\sigma(\bar{\lambda}, k, q)]}{\sigma(\bar{\lambda}, k, q)} - y(\bar{\lambda}, K, q) + i^* b.$$

Linearize this expression for $\dot{b}(t)$ around the steady state and substitute for $q(t) - \bar{q}$ to derive the linear differential equation

$$\dot{b}(t) = \Omega(K_0 - \overline{K})e^{\mu_1 t} + i^*[b(t) - \overline{b}],$$

where:

$$\Omega \equiv \frac{1}{\sigma}\left[(\beta\sigma_K - \sigma y_K) + (\beta\sigma_q - \sigma y_q)\frac{\mu_1}{I_q}\right], \text{ and}$$

$$\beta \equiv Z'(\sigma) + i^* b - y.$$

Assuming the initial condition $b(0) = b_0$, the solution to this differential equation is

$$b(t) = \overline{b} + \frac{\Omega(K_0 - \overline{K})}{\mu_1 - i^*}e^{\mu_1 t} + \left[b_0 - \overline{b} - \frac{\Omega(K_0 - \overline{K})}{\mu_1 - i^*}\right]e^{i^* t}.$$

Given this solution for $b(t)$, the only way the consumer's transversality condition can hold is to impose the following relationship between $\overline{b}$ and the initial values b_0 and K_0:

$$\overline{b} = b_0 + \frac{\Omega}{\mu_1 - i^*}(\overline{K} - K_0).$$

Exercise 12.6

Maurice Obstfeld presents a small open economy model, which is based on the behavior of an optimizing representative agent, in an article entitled "Macroeconomic Policy, Exchange-Rate Dynamics, and Optimal Asset Accumulation" (1981, *Journal of Political Economy*, 89, 1142-61). A unique feature of this model is the incorporation of preferences introduced by Uzawa in 1968 (referenced in the text), which postulate that the consumer's discount rate is an increasing, convex function of utility. Specifically, the representative agent in this small open economy chooses consumption (c) and real money balances (m) so as to

$$\max \int_0^\infty U[c(t), m(t)]e^{-\Delta(t)}dt$$

s.t. $\dot{a}(t) = ra(t) + \tau(t) - c(t) - [\pi(t) + r]m(t),$

where:

$a(t) \equiv$ real wealth,

$r \equiv$ the real interest rate on internationally traded bonds,

$\tau(t) \equiv$ real transfers from the government, and

$\pi(t) \equiv$ the expected inflation rate.

The consumer's discount factor depends on utility in the following way:

$$\Delta(t) \equiv \int_0^t \delta\{U[c(s),m(s)]\}ds.$$

We assume that the function $\delta(\cdot)$ possesses the following properties:

$\delta'(U) > 0$, $\delta''(U) > 0$, and $\delta(U) - U\delta'(U) > 0$.

Derive the necessary conditions for a solution to the consumer's optimization problem, assuming the agent takes r, $\tau(t)$ and $\pi(t)$ as exogenously given.

Hint: Use the relationship $d\Delta = \delta(U)dt$ to make a change of variable for dt, thus converting the problem to "psychological time" (i.e. time measured in increments of Δ).

Solution: After making the indicated change of variable, we can rewrite the consumer's problem as

$$\max \int_0^\infty \frac{U(c,m)}{\delta[U(c,m)]} e^{-\Delta} d\Delta$$

s.t. $\dfrac{da}{d\Delta} = \dfrac{ra + \tau - c - (\pi + r)m}{\delta[U(c,m)]}.$

The current value Hamiltonian for this problem is

$$H^* = \frac{U(c,m)}{\delta[U(c,m)]} + \lambda \frac{ra + \tau - c - (\pi + r)m}{\delta[U(c,m)]},$$

and it gives rise to two static optimality conditions and a costate equation.

$$U_c - \left(\frac{\delta'}{\delta}\right)\{U(c,m) + \lambda[ra + \tau - c - (\pi+r)m]\}U_c = \lambda$$

$$U_m - \left(\frac{\delta'}{\delta}\right)\{U(c,m) + \lambda[ra + \tau - c - (\pi+r)m]\}U_m = \lambda(\pi+r)$$

$$\frac{d\lambda}{d\Delta} = \lambda\left(\frac{\delta - r}{\delta}\right)$$

By the chain rule, the costate equation may be written as a differential equation in ordinary time.

$$\dot{\lambda} = \lambda\{\delta[U(c.m)] - r\}$$

The last equation is identical to the costate equation we would find with ordinary preferences, except that δ is time-varying. This is a significant difference, because it means there is a well-defined steady state for the marginal utility of wealth. We don't have to impose an arbitrary constraint of the form $\bar{\delta} = r$.

Exercise 12.7

Obstfeld develops the model presented in Exercise 12.6 into a complete, general equilibrium monetary growth model. He assumes that the central bank allows the nominal money stock to grow at a fixed rate $(\dot{M}/M \equiv \mu)$, while government expenditures (g) and central bank foreign reserves (R) are constant, and government transfers (τ) vary so as to balance the budget. The central bank earns the world interest rate on its reserves, so the government budget constraint takes the form

$$\tau(t) = \mu m(t) + rR - g.$$

The real money stock is defined as

$$m(t) \equiv \frac{M(t)}{P(t)},$$

where P is the price level and M is the nominal money stock. Private sector real wealth (a) consists of the net present value of a constant, exogenous flow of income (y/r) plus holdings of foreign bonds (F) and real money balances (m):

$$a(t) = \frac{y}{r} + F(t) + m(t).$$

This is a perfect-foresight model, so both the actual and expected rates of inflation are given by

$$\pi(t) \equiv \frac{\dot{P}(t)}{P(t)}.$$

Derive a linearized dynamic system describing the evolution of real consumption, real money balances and real foreign bond holdings along a perfect-foresight equilibrium path. You may assume the existence of a unique, saddlepoint-stable solution.

Hint: Take the ratio of the two static optimality conditions to derive an expression for the marginal rate of substitution of goods for real balances,

$$x(c,m) \equiv \frac{U_m(c,m)}{U_c(c,m)} = \pi + r.$$

Use this relationship to eliminate the nominal variable, π, from the dynamic system.

Solution: The linearized dynamic system is shown below, with over-bars to indicate the fact that the linearization is about the steady state point $(\bar{c}, \bar{m}, \bar{F})$. Subscripts denote partial derivatives.

$$\begin{bmatrix} \dot{c}(t) \\ \dot{m}(t) \\ \dot{F}(t) \end{bmatrix} = \begin{bmatrix} \overline{\psi}_c & \overline{\psi}_m & \overline{\psi}_F \\ -\overline{m}\overline{x}_c & -\overline{m}\overline{x}_m & 0 \\ -1 & 0 & r \end{bmatrix} \begin{bmatrix} c(t) - \bar{c} \\ m(t) - \bar{m} \\ F(t) - \bar{F} \end{bmatrix}$$

$$\psi(c,m,F+R) = \frac{1}{\lambda_c}\left\{\lambda\left[\delta(U) - r\right] - \lambda_m \dot{m} - \lambda_F \dot{F}\right\}$$

$$\lambda(c,m,F+R) = \frac{(\delta - U\delta')U_c}{\delta + \left\{y + r(F+R) + \left[\mu + r - x(c,m)\right]m - c - g\right\}\delta' \cdot U_c}$$

Obstfeld presents all of the partial derivative expressions and proves the existence of a unique, stable saddle path solution (provided $\mu + r > 0$). c and m are jump variables, and the system has one negative root to correspond with the sluggish state variable, F.

13 An Introduction to Endogenous Growth Models

Exercise 13.1

Consider a centralized economy, in which output is produced according to the constant returns to scale production function: $Y(t) = F[K(t), \theta(t)L(t)]$. The effective labor supply is given by θL, where L is the population and θ is a productivity factor. The rate of population growth and the rate of labor-augmenting technical progress are exogenously given constants:

$$\frac{\dot{L}(t)}{L(t)} = n, \text{ and } \frac{\dot{\theta}(t)}{\theta(t)} = \mu.$$

There is no government sector in this model, so the aggregate market clearance condition is simply $Y(t) = C(t) + \dot{K}(t)$. Express the market clearing condition in intensive form (i.e. per unit of effective labor), using the following notation:

$$k(t) = \frac{K(t)}{\theta(t)L(t)}, \quad c(t) = \frac{C(t)}{\theta(t)L(t)}, \text{ and } y(t) = \frac{Y(t)}{\theta(t)L(t)}.$$

Solve the infinite horizon planner's problem, subject to this market clearing condition, and assuming the following logarithmic felicity function:

$$U\left[\frac{C(t)}{L(t)}\right] = U[\theta(t)c(t)] = ln[\theta(t)c(t)].$$

Hint: Use the homogeneity of the aggregate production function to derive an intensive form production function, $y(t) = f[k(t)]$.

Solution: The optimal equations of motion are:

$$\dot{c} = c[f'(k) - (\beta + n + \mu)], \text{ and}$$

$$\dot{k} = f(k) - c - (\mu + n)k ,$$

where β is the planner's discount factor. The transversality condition is

$$\lim_{t \to \infty} e^{-\beta t} \frac{k}{c} = 0 .$$

Exercise 13.2

Assuming the Inada conditions $(f'(0) = \infty, f'(\infty) = 0)$ hold, the dynamic system derived in exercise 13.1 has a steady state $(\bar{c}, \bar{k})$ in the ratios of consumption and capital to the *effective* labor supply. Derive the stable solution to a linearized approximation of this system. How do the ratios of consumption and capital to the *actual* labor supply (i.e. the population) evolve once the steady state in c and k has been reached?

Hint: Use the transversality condition to argue that the coefficient on the unstable portion of the solution must equal zero.

Solution: Letting η_1 denote the negative characteristic root of the linearized system, we find the following stable solution:

$$\begin{bmatrix} c(t) \\ k(t) \end{bmatrix} = \begin{bmatrix} \bar{c} \\ \bar{k} \end{bmatrix} + (k_0 - \bar{k}) \begin{bmatrix} \bar{c} f''(\bar{k})/\eta_1 \\ 1 \end{bmatrix} e^{\eta_1 t} \xrightarrow[t \to \infty]{} \begin{bmatrix} \bar{c} \\ \bar{k} \end{bmatrix}.$$

Once c and k reach their steady state values, C/L and K/L continue to grow, due to exogenous technical progress. Specifically, they evolve according to the following pair of equations.

$$\begin{bmatrix} C(t)/L(t) \\ K(t)/L(t) \end{bmatrix} = \begin{bmatrix} \bar{c} \theta_0 e^{\mu t} \\ \bar{k} \theta_0 e^{\mu t} \end{bmatrix}$$

Exercise 13.3

Suppose the representative agent in an economy has lifetime utility function

$$\int_0^\infty e^{-bt} \ln[C(t)] dt ,$$

where b is a subjective discount factor and $C(t)$ is the time t consumption flow. There is no population growth. Output is produced according to the linear technology:

$$Y(t) = F[K(t)] = aK(t),$$

and the capital stock evolves according to the equation

$$\dot{K}(t) = aK(t) - C(t) - \delta K(t),$$

where δ is the constant rate of depreciation.

Set up and solve the representative agent's dynamic optimization problem. Draw a phase diagram in (C, K) space, assuming that $a > b + \delta$. Derive reduced form equations for $K(t)$, $C(t)$ and $Y(t)$, which satisfy all optimality conditions (including the transversality condition).

Hint: Postulate the existence of a balanced growth path, along which:

$$\mu = \frac{\dot{K}}{K} = \frac{\dot{C}}{C} = \frac{\dot{Y}}{Y},$$

and solve for this growth rate.

Solution: There is no steady state, as is evident from the phase diagram shown below. There are no transitional dynamics in this economy. Starting from the initial capital stock, $K(0)$, we jump onto the balanced growth path.

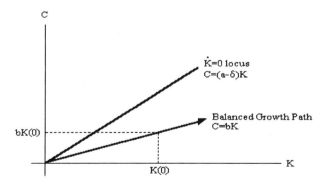

Along the balanced growth path, K, C and Y all grow at the same rate, $\mu = a - (b+\delta)$. The reduced form equations describing the evolution of these variables are:

$K(t) = K(0)e^{\mu t}$,

$C(t) = C(0)e^{\mu t} = bK(0)e^{\mu t}$, and

$Y(t) = Y(0)e^{\mu t} = aK(0)e^{\mu t}$.

Exercise 13.4

Redo Exercise 13.3, only this time assume the following aggregate technology.

$$Y(t) = F[K(t)] = aK(t) + 2K(t)^{\frac{1}{2}}$$

As before, assume that $a > b + \delta$. Draw the phase diagram for this economy, but don't try to find analytical solutions for K, C and Y. The equations of motion are nonlinear, and it makes no sense to solve a linear approximation to the system (why?).

Hint: This time, look for an asymptotic balanced growth path, along which the growth rates of K, C and Y all converge to a common value as $t \to \infty$.

Solution: The equilibrium growth rate, $\mu = a - (b+\delta)$, is the same as in Exercise 11.3. However, in this case the economy only approaches this growth rate asymptotically as $t \to \infty$. The phase diagram is shown below.

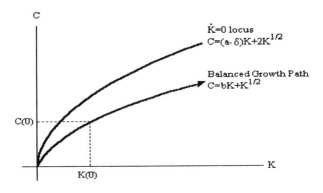

Asymptotically, the slope of the $\dot{K}=0$ locus $(a-\delta)$ is greater than the limiting slope of the balanced growth path (b).

Exercise 13.5

Consider an economy operated by a central planner, who maximizes

$$W = \int_0^\infty \frac{1}{\gamma} C(t)^\gamma e^{-\beta t} dt,$$

subject to the resource constraint

$$\dot{K}(t) = \alpha K(t) - C(t) - G(t) \quad, \quad \alpha > 0,$$

where α is the constant marginal product of capital. Suppose the government sets its expenditures in accordance with the rule $G(t) = gC(t)$, where g is a constant. Derive the equilibrium growth rate of the economy and the equilibrium consumption-to-capital ratio. Show how the government expenditure parameter (g) impacts on these aspects of the equilibrium.

Hint: Postulate a balanced growth path, and solve for the rate of growth of C, K, Y and G along this path. The transversality condition can be used to establish the sign of the marginal effect of g on C/K.

Solution: The equilibrium growth rate $\left(\phi \equiv \dot{C}/C = \dot{K}/K = \dot{Y}/Y = \dot{G}/G\right)$ and consumption-to-capital ratio $(\mu \equiv C/K)$ are given by the following expressions:

$$\phi = \frac{\beta - \alpha}{\gamma - 1}, \text{ and } \mu = \frac{\alpha\gamma - \beta}{(1+g)(\gamma - 1)}.$$

The government expenditure parameter (g) does not impact the growth rate (ϕ). However, it does affect the equilibrium consumption-to-capital ratio (μ). We can show that μ varies inversely with g, if $\beta > \alpha\gamma$.

$$\frac{d\mu}{dg} = \frac{\alpha\gamma - \beta}{(1-\gamma)(1+g)^2} < 0 \text{ if } \beta > \alpha\gamma$$

The inequality $\beta > \alpha\gamma$ is a necessary condition for the transversality condition,

$$\lim_{t\to\infty} e^{-\beta t}\frac{C(t)^{\gamma-1}}{1+g}K(t)=0,$$

to be satisfied. In order to see this, substitute the solutions for C(t) and K(t) into the above transversality condition and show that:

$$\lim_{t\to\infty} e^{-\beta t}\frac{C(t)^{\gamma-1}}{1+g}K(t) = \lim_{t\to\infty}\frac{(\mu K_0)^{\gamma-1}K_0}{1+g}e^{(\phi\gamma-\beta)t}.$$

The latter expression is zero only if $\phi\gamma-\beta<0$, and it's easy to show that $\beta>\alpha\gamma$ is a necessary condition for $\phi\gamma-\beta<0$ to hold.

Exercise 13.6

Consider the decentralized economy corresponding to the centrally planned economy of the previous exercise. Demonstrate that the first best optimum can be achieved by setting a consumption tax rate $\omega = g$ and leaving capital untaxed. Recall from exercise 13.5 that $G = gC$.

Hint: Assume that firms rent capital from consumers and install it without adjustment costs.

Solution: The representative consumer seeks to

$$\max \int_0^\infty \frac{C(t)^\gamma}{\gamma}e^{-\beta t}dt$$

s.t. $\dot{B}(t)+\dot{K}(t)=(1-\tau_K)rK(t)+iB(t)-(1+\omega)C(t),$

where $B(t)$ is the stock of government bonds held by the consumer at time t. Although the rental rate on capital (r) and the interest rate on government bonds (i) could vary over time, they turn out to be constant in equilibrium. In fact, firm profit maximization and the absence of arbitrage opportunities will ensure that

$$\frac{i}{1-\tau_K}=r=\alpha=MP_K$$

at all times. The consumer's optimality conditions are (in addition to the flow budget constraint stated as part of the problem):

$$\frac{\dot{C}}{C} = \frac{\beta - (1-\tau_K)r}{\gamma - 1},$$

$i = (1-\tau_K)r$, and

$$\lim_{t \to \infty} e^{-\beta t} \frac{C^{\gamma-1}}{1+\omega} K = \lim_{t \to \infty} e^{-\beta t} \frac{C^{\gamma-1}}{1+\omega} B = 0$$

Finally, we have the following government budget constraint:

$$\dot{B}(t) = iB(t) + G - \omega C - \tau_K rK.$$

This last condition may be satisfied by setting $\omega = g$ and never issuing any government bonds $(B(t) = \dot{B}(t) = 0 \, \forall t)$. Substitute this condition and the firm's profit maximization condition $(r = \alpha)$ into the consumer's optimality conditions. We end up with the same equations of motion for C, K and G and the same boundary conditions (i.e. same initial and transversality conditions) as in Exercise 13.5. Thus, a balanced budget policy, with government expenditures financed solely by a consumption tax (at rate $\omega = g$), leads to a decentralized equilibrium with the first-best allocation of resources.

Exercise 13.7

In his 1991 article entitled, "Long-run Policy Analysis and Long-run Growth," (*Journal of Political Economy*, 99, 500-521) Rebelo describes a two sector endogenous growth model in which investment goods, $I(t)$, sell for price $p(t)$ relative to the numeraire consumption good, $C(t)$. A representative firm rents capital, $Z(t)$, and the fixed supply of land, T, from the representative consumer for prices $x(t)$ and $s(t)$ respectively. The firm uses these inputs to produce consumption goods and investment goods according to the technologies

$C(t) = B[\phi Z(t)]^\alpha T^{1-\alpha}$, and

$I(t) = A(1-\phi)Z(t)$,

where ϕ is the fraction of capital dedicated to the production of consumption goods, while A and B are fixed technical parameters. The profit maximizing firm sells its output to a representative consumer, who seeks to

Chapter 13

$$\max \int_0^\infty e^{-\rho t} \frac{C(t)^{1-\sigma} - 1}{1-\sigma} dt$$

s.t. $C(t) + p(t)I(t) = x(t)Z(t) + s(t)T$, and

$$\dot{Z}(t) = I(t) - \delta Z(t),$$

where δ is the constant rate of capital depreciation. There is no government in this economy. All wealth is held by the consumer in the form of capital or land.

Derive the equilibrium growth rates for capital, consumption and the relative price of investment goods. Also, determine the equilibrium share of capital devoted to the production of consumption goods.

Hint: Consumption and the capital stock grow at the same rate in equilibrium, but only when they are expressed in a common unit of value (i.e only after accounting for a possible trend in the price of capital relative to consumption goods).

Solution:

$$g_Z \equiv \frac{\dot{Z}}{Z} = \frac{A - \delta - \rho}{1 - \alpha + \alpha\sigma}; \quad g_C \equiv \frac{\dot{C}}{C} = \alpha g_Z; \quad g_p \equiv \frac{\dot{p}}{p} = (\alpha - 1)g_Z; \quad \phi = 1 - \frac{\delta + g_Z}{A}$$

14 Continuous-Time Stochastic Optimization

Exercise 14.1

This exercise and the next one are taken from *Options, Futures and Other Derivative Securities, Second Edition,* by John C. Hull (1993, Prentice-Hall). They are intended to provide the reader some practice in applying Ito's lemma.

A common model for non-dividend-paying stocks posits that the stock price, S, follows a geometric Brownian motion process with a fixed drift rate, μ, and a fixed proportional diffusion rate, σ. Mathematically, we write this process as follows:

$dS = \mu S dt + \sigma S dz$,

where dz is a standard Wiener process (i.e., $dz \sim N(0, dt)$ in independent increments). Derive the stochastic process followed by the natural logarithm of the stock price.

Hint: Let $G(S,t) = ln(S)$ and apply equation (14.9') in the text.

Solution: $dG = \dfrac{dS}{S} = \left(\mu - \dfrac{\sigma^2}{2}\right)dt + \sigma dz$.

Exercise 14.2

Assume a non-dividend-paying stock obeys the geometric Brownian motion process given in Exercise 14.1. Let r represent the constant risk-free rate of interest, and let $F(t)$ represent the price of a forward contract committing the holder to purchase a share of the underlying stock at time $T > t$. In order to prevent arbitrage opportunities, the following relationship must hold between the forward price, F, and the price of the underlying stock, S:

$$F(t) = S(t)e^{r(T-t)}.$$

Derive the stochastic process followed by the forward price.

Hint: Apply Ito's lemma.

Solution: $dF = (\mu - r)Fdt + \sigma F dz$.

Thus, the forward price also obeys a geometric Brownian motion process, with a proportional drift rate that differs from that of the underlying stock price by an amount equal to the constant risk-free rate of interest.

Exercise 14.3

This exercise is an example presented by Avinash K. Dixit and Robert S. Pindyck in their book *Investment Under Certainty* (1994, Princeton University Press). Suppose x and y follow correlated geometric Brownian motions:

$dx = \alpha_x x dt + \sigma_x x dz_x$, and

$dy = \alpha_y y dt + \sigma_y y dz_y$.

The standard Wiener processes dz_x and dz_y have covariance ρ per unit of time. Solve for the stochastic processes governing the evolution of $F(x, y) = xy$ and $G(x, y) = ln(xy) = ln(F)$.

Hint: If the appropriate form of equation (14.9) is not obvious to you, take a second order Taylor approximation to the given functions, and apply the appropriate differential multiplication rules (e.g. $(dt)^2 = 0$).

Solution:

$$dF = (\alpha_x + \alpha_y + \rho\sigma_x\sigma_y)Fdt + (\sigma_x dz_x + \sigma_y dz_y)F$$

$$dG = \left(\alpha_x + \alpha_y - \frac{1}{2}\sigma_x^2 - \frac{1}{2}\sigma_y^2\right)dt + \sigma_x dz_x + \sigma_y dz_y$$

Exercise 14.4

The following model was developed by Robert Merton (1969, *Review of Economics and Statistics*, 51, 247-257) and is presented as an example by Kamien and Schwartz in *Dynamic Optimization: The Calculus of Variations and Optimal Control in Economics and Management*, Second Edition (1991, North-Holland). An individual chooses consumption, $C(t)$, and the fraction, $\omega(t)$, of wealth, $W(t)$, to hold in a risky asset at each instant, so as to:

$$\max \quad E_0 \int_0^\infty e^{-rt} \frac{C(t)^b}{b} dt \quad ; \quad b<1, r>0$$

s.t. $\quad dW = [s(1-\omega)W + a\omega W - C]dt + \omega W \sigma dz \quad ; \quad W(0) = W_0.$

We assume that the expected return on the risky asset exceeds the riskless return $(a > s)$. dz represents a standard Wiener process, while σ is the volatility rate of the risky asset.

Derive the stochastic Bellman equation for this control problem. Use the first order conditions associated with the maximization problem on the right hand side of the Bellman equation, to derive expressions for C and ω that depend on wealth, as well as the value function and/or its derivatives.

Hint: Use the autonomous form of the stochastic Bellman equation, as given by equation (14.15') in the text.

Solution: Letting $V(W)$ represent the value function, the stochastic Bellman Equation takes the form

$$rV(W) = \max_{C,\omega} \left\{ \frac{C^b}{b} + V'(W)[s(1-\omega)W + a\omega W - C] + \frac{1}{2}\omega^2 W^2 \sigma^2 V''(W) \right\}.$$

The following expressions satisfy the first order conditions associated with the maximization problem on the right hand side of the stochastic Bellman equation:

$$C = [V'(W)]^{\frac{1}{b-1}}, \text{ and}$$

$$\omega = \frac{V'(W)(s-a)}{\sigma^2 W V''(W)}.$$

Note: If you have difficulty deriving the stochastic Bellman equation, consult one or more of the references on stochastic calculus, which are provided at the start of Section 14.2 of the text.

Exercise 14.5

Continuing with Exercise 14.4, use the method of undetermined coefficients to derive reduced form expressions for C, ω, and the value function, $V(W)$.

Hint: The value function will take the form $V(W) = AW^b$, where A is a coefficient to be determined, so as to satisfy the stochastic Bellman equation.

Solution:

$$C = W(Ab)^{\frac{1}{b-1}},$$

$$\omega = \frac{a-s}{(1-b)\sigma^2}, \text{ and}$$

$$V(W) = AW^b,$$

where:

$$A = \frac{1}{b}\left\{\frac{1}{1-b}\left[r - sb - \frac{(s-a)^2 b}{2\sigma^2(1-b)}\right]\right\}^{b-1}.$$

Exercise 14.6

The following model of investment was developed by Andrew Abel and Janice Eberly ("A Unified Model of Investment Under Uncertainty", *American Economic Review*, December 1994, 84, 1369-1384). The value of the firm at time t is given by

$$V[K(t),\varepsilon(t)] = \max_{I,d} E_t \int_0^\infty e^{-rs} \left\{\begin{matrix}\pi[K(t+s),\varepsilon(t+s)] \\ -d(t+s)C[I(t+s),K(t+s)]\end{matrix}\right\} ds,$$

where:

$K(t) \equiv$ the firm's capital stock at time t,

$\varepsilon(t) \equiv$ a shock to the firm's time t profits,

$I(t) \equiv$ the rate of investment at time t,

$d(t) \equiv$ an indicator variable:

($d = 0$ when $I = 0$; $d = 1$ when $I \neq 0$),

$\pi(K, \varepsilon) \equiv$ the firm's instantaneous profit function,

$C(I, K) \equiv$ the firm's investment cost function, and

$r \equiv$ constant (exogenously given) discount rate.

The profit function, $\pi(K, \varepsilon)$, reflects optimal choices for all costlessly adjustable inputs (e.g., labor). We assume this function has the following properties:

$\pi_K > 0$, $\pi_\varepsilon > 0$ and $\pi_{KK} < 0$.

Shocks to the firm's profits may reflect changes in technology, output prices or costlessly adjustable input prices. These shocks follow the diffusion process

$$d\varepsilon = \mu(\varepsilon)dt + \sigma(\varepsilon)dz,$$

while the capital stock evolves according to the deterministic process

$$dK = (I - \delta K)dt,$$

where δ is the fixed rate of capital depreciation.

Write down the current value stochastic Bellman equation for the firm's wealth maximization problem, which is subject to the dynamic processes for ε and K. Derive the optimality condition for investment, assuming for the time being that $d(t) = 1 \, \forall t$ is optimal.

Hint: Define the marginal value of a unit of installed capital as $q \equiv V_K(K, \varepsilon)$, where $V(K, \varepsilon)$ is the current value function. Use this definition when writing down the stochastic Bellman equation.

Solution: The stochastic Bellman equation is

$$rV(K,\varepsilon) = \max_{I,d}\left\{\pi(K,\varepsilon) - dC(I,K) + q(I - \delta K) + \mu V_\varepsilon + \frac{1}{2}\sigma^2 V_{\varepsilon\varepsilon}\right\}.$$

At times when the firm finds that it is optimal to set $d = 1$, the optimality condition for investment is simply

$$C_I\left[I^*(q,K), K\right] = q,$$

where $I^*(q, K)$ denotes the optimal level of investment. Note that the parameters of the profit function do not enter the investment function directly, although they may affect I^* indirectly through q.

Exercise 14.7

Continuing with the model presented in Exercise 14.6, suppose the investment cost function is composed of three parts. Specifically,

$$C(I,K) = P(I) + A(I,K) + f,$$

where:

$P(I)$ ≡ the purchase/sales price of capital goods,

$A(I,K)$ ≡ the variable adjustment/installation costs, and

f ≡ the fixed investment cost per unit of time.

If capital goods have some firm-specific attributes and/or there is a "lemons" problem in the market for used capital goods, we would expect that the firm must pay a higher price for capital than it can charge when selling capital. We can specify the form of $P(I)$ to capture this aspect of the firm's investment problem. A very simple example of this would be to let

$$P(I) = \begin{cases} I & \text{if } I \geq 0 \\ (1/2)I & \text{if } I < 0 \end{cases}.$$

A common specification for adjustment costs is the convex, linearly homogeneous function

$$A(I,K) = \frac{1}{2}\frac{I^2}{K}.$$

Overall, we have the following investment cost function:

$$C(I,K) = \begin{cases} I + \dfrac{1}{2}\dfrac{I^2}{K} + f & \text{if } I \geq 0 \\ \dfrac{1}{2}I + \dfrac{1}{2}\dfrac{I^2}{K} + f & \text{if } I < 0 \end{cases}.$$

Of course, if the firm chooses to neither invest or disinvest (i.e. chooses to set $I = 0$), then $d = 0$, and total investment costs are zero at that instant.

Describe the firm's optimal investment decision rule, as a function of the shadow value of capital, q.

Hint: Separately consider the following two cases.

Case 1: $I = 0, d = 0$, and

Case 2: $I \neq 0, d = 1$.

Think about when the firm should choose Case 1 and when it should choose Case 2.

Solution: The optimal decision rule for the firm is to set

$$\frac{I^*}{K} = \begin{cases} q - 1 > 0 & \text{if } q > 1 \\ 0 & \text{if } 1/2 \leq q \leq 1 \\ q - 1/2 < 0 & \text{if } q < 1/2 \end{cases}.$$

15 A Stochastic Intertemporal Model of a Small Open Economy

Exercise 15.1

This exercise is based on some expressions derived by René Stulz in his 1981 article, "A Model of International Asset Pricing" (*Journal of Financial Economics*, 9, 383-406). Suppose a share of Sony stock costs I* yen, pays no dividends, and generates yen-denominated returns in the form of capital gains, according to the following geometric Brownian motion process:

$$\frac{dI}{I^*} = \mu_{I^*} dt + \sigma_{I^*} dz_{I^*}.$$

An American investor can buy shares of Sony, but she must first trade dollars for yen at the exchange rate e. We assume the law of one price applies to Sony shares and denote the dollar price by D=eI*. The spot exchange rate also evolves stochastically according to

$$\frac{de}{e} = \mu_e dt + \sigma_e dz_e.$$

Derive the stochastic process for the dollar price of Sony shares. Also, derive an expression for the excess dollar return on Sony shares, assuming the investment is financed by borrowing yen at the Japanese (nominally) riskless interest rate R^*. To be clear, R^* is the instantaneous rate of return on Japanese bonds that sell for B^* yen, so

$$\frac{dB^*}{B^*} = R^* dt.$$

Hint: Think of a zero net investment portfolio, which is long in Sony stock and short in Japanese bonds. What is the instantaneous dollar-denominated return on such a portfolio?

Solution: The American investor's dollar rate of return on Sony stock is given by

$$\frac{dD}{D} = \frac{d(eI^*)}{eI^*} = \frac{dI^*}{I^*} + \frac{de}{e} + \left(\frac{de}{e}\right)\left(\frac{dI^*}{I^*}\right),$$

while the dollar return on her bond investments is

$$-\frac{d(eB^*)}{eB^*} = -\frac{dB^*}{B^*} - \frac{de}{e} - \left(\frac{de}{e}\right)\left(\frac{dB^*}{B^*}\right).$$

As long as the portfolio is continuously rebalanced, so the number of dollars worth of Sony stock plus the number of dollars worth of Japanese bonds add to zero, we can combine the two rates of return to derive the instantaneous rate of return on the Sony stock / Japanese bonds portfolio.

$$\frac{dD}{D} - \frac{d(eB^*)}{eB^*} = \left(\mu_{I^*} - R^* + \rho_{eI^*}\sigma_e\sigma_{I^*}\right)dt + \sigma_{I^*}dz_{I^*}$$

The expected excess return on this portfolio is

$$\mu_{I^*} - R^* + \rho_{eI^*}\sigma_e\sigma_{I^*},$$

whereas the expected excess return to a Japanese investor is just

$$\mu_{I^*} - R^*.$$

The difference is explained by the covariation of the price of Sony shares with the dollar / yen exchange rate. It is not explained by exchange rate variation per se.

Exercise 15.2

René Stulz analyzes the optimal consumption and asset allocation choices of an individual who may hold foreign and domestic assets (including currencies) in a 1984 article entitled, "Currency Preferences, Purchasing Power Risks, and the Determination of Exchange Rates in an Optimizing Model"

(*Journal of Money, Credit and Banking*, 16, 302-316). The next few exercises relate to the optimal choices of an individual investor in a slightly simplified version of the model. Stulz extends the model to derive general equilibrium results.

The individual must decide how much to consume (and thereby how much to save) and how to allocate his portfolio at each instant in time. There are six assets available to him for investment purposes: capital (K), domestic real balances (m), foreign real balances (m^*), domestic bonds (b), foreign bonds (b^*) and an asset that is riskless in real terms (Y). Currencies and bonds are denominated in money terms, but they can be converted into consumption goods (the numeraire) at a rate that the investor takes as given. Specifically, let

$$m = \Pi M, \quad m^* = \Pi^* M^*, \quad b = \Pi B, \quad \text{and} \quad b^* = \Pi^* B^*,$$

where M, M^*, B and B^* represent the nominal value of domestic and foreign money and bond holdings, and Π and Π^* are defined as follows:

$\Pi \equiv$ the consumption good price of one unit of domestic money.

$\Pi^* \equiv$ the consumption good price of one unit of foreign money.

There is only one type of consumption good, so Π^* implicitly reflects a nominal exchange rate. We assume the investor takes the following stochastic processes for Π and Π^* as exogenously given:

$$\frac{d\Pi}{\Pi} = \mu_\Pi dt + \sigma_\Pi dz_\Pi, \text{ and}$$

$$\frac{d\Pi^*}{\Pi^*} = \mu_{\Pi^*} dt + \sigma_{\Pi^*} dz_{\Pi^*}.$$

He also takes as given that

$$\frac{dK}{K} = \mu_K dt + \sigma_K dz_K,$$

$$\frac{dB}{B} = R dt, \quad \frac{dB^*}{B^*} = R^* dt, \quad \text{and} \quad \frac{dY}{Y} = r dt.$$

All of the "dz's" in this model represent ordinary Wiener processes, which may be correlated with one another. Note that Y provides a riskless real return, while B and B^* are subject to purchasing power risk, even though they pay fixed nominal returns.

Write down the individual's stock and flow wealth constraints in real terms, applying Ito's lemma where it is appropriate to do so.

Hint: One convenient way to express the flow constraint is in "share form" (i.e. in relation to total real wealth, W). Consumption choices can be expressed as a ratio to total wealth in this form of the constraint.

Solution: The stock constraint is obvious enough. Expressing it in real terms, we have

$$W = K + \Pi M + \Pi^* M^* + \Pi B + \Pi^* B^* + Y.$$

When we convert this into differential form, we must account for the effect of consumption, which is a flow variable.

$$dW = dK + d(\Pi M) + d(\Pi^* M^*) + d(\Pi B) + d(\Pi^* B^*) + dY + dC$$

The sign on dC doesn't look right, but I'll explain it in a moment. We can divide through by W and multiply each term by one, expressed in a convenient way, which leads to the following share form of the flow wealth constraint:

$$\frac{dW}{W} = \omega_K \frac{dK}{K} + \omega_M \frac{d(\Pi M)}{\Pi M} + \omega_{M^*} \frac{d(\Pi^* M^*)}{\Pi^* M^*} + \omega_B \frac{d(\Pi B)}{\Pi B}$$

$$+ \omega_{B^*} \frac{d(\Pi^* B^*)}{\Pi^* B^*} + \omega_Y \frac{dY}{Y} + c \frac{dC}{C},$$

where portfolio shares $(\omega's)$ and the consumption to wealth ratio (c) are defined as follows:

$$\omega_K \equiv \frac{K}{W}, \quad \omega_M \equiv \frac{\Pi M}{W}, \quad \omega_{M^*} \equiv \frac{\Pi^* M^*}{W}, \quad \omega_B \equiv \frac{\Pi B}{W}, \quad \omega_{B^*} \equiv \frac{\Pi^* B^*}{W},$$

$$\omega_Y \equiv \frac{Y}{W}, \text{ and } c \equiv \frac{C}{W}.$$

Substitute the given stochastic processes into this equation, impose the stock wealth constraint $\left(\omega_Y = 1 - \omega_K - \omega_M - \omega_{M^*} - \omega_B - \omega_{B^*}\right)$ and gather terms, leading to the flow wealth constraint shown below:

$$dW = W\mu_w dt + W\sigma_w dz_w,$$

where:

$$\mu_w = \omega_K(\mu_K - r) + \omega_M(\mu_\Pi - r) + \omega_{M^*}(\mu_{\Pi^*} - r) + \omega_B(R + \mu_\Pi - r)$$

$$+ \omega_{B^*}\left(R^* + \mu_{\Pi^*} - r\right) + r - c, \text{ and}$$

$$\sigma_w dz_w = \omega_K \sigma_K dz_K + (\omega_M + \omega_B)\sigma_\Pi dz_\Pi + (\omega_{M^*} + \omega_{B^*})\sigma_{\Pi^*} dz_{\Pi^*}.$$

μ_w is the drift rate of real wealth, and it is expressed as a function of portfolio shares, r, c and expected real excess returns on risky assets. σ_w is the instantaneous volatility of wealth, and it depends on portfolio shares and the underlying volatility parameters. Finally, I have used the fact that

$$\frac{dC}{C} = -dt.$$

That is, consumption is an "investment" that is certain to yield a financial return of negative 100%.

Exercise 15.3

Suppose an individual investor chooses consumption (as a proportion of his wealth) and portfolio weights so as to maximize his expected lifetime utility, subject to the flow wealth constraint derived in exercise 15.2. Lifetime utility at time zero is given by

$$U = \int_0^\infty e^{-\rho t} \frac{1}{\gamma} S^\gamma dt,$$

where S represents "consumption services," which are produced from real consumption goods and real (domestic and foreign) money balances according to the following technology:

$$S = C^{\delta}\left[a(\Pi M)^{\beta} + (1-a)\left(\Pi^{*}M^{*}\right)^{\beta}\right]^{\frac{1-\delta}{\beta}}.$$

Define the current value function for this investor's control problem and write down the associated stochastic Bellman equation. Derive the first order conditions that must be satisfied by any solution to the problem.

Hint: Transform S into "share form" and write the resulting expression in the form $S = W f(c, \omega_M, \omega_{M^*}; a, \beta, \delta)$.

Solution: The consumption services function may be written as

$$S = Wc^{\delta}\left[a\omega_M^{\beta} + (1-a)\omega_{M^*}^{\beta}\right]^{\frac{1-\delta}{\beta}}.$$

We define the current value function as

$$V(W,\cdot) \equiv \max_{c,\omega's} E_0 \int_0^{\infty} e^{-\rho t} \frac{1}{\gamma} S(W,\cdot)^{\gamma} dt$$

s.t. $dW = W\mu_w dt + W\sigma_w dz_w$,

where μ_w and $\sigma_w dz_w$ are defined in exercise 15.2. The notation $V(W,\cdot)$ and $S(W,\cdot)$ reflects the fact that these functions also depend on control variables and exogenous parameters. With this in mind, we can suppress these other arguments entirely, when it is convenient to do so. The problem is autonomous, and we have arbitrarily set it up to be solved at time $t = 0$. $V(W)$ is appropriately referred to as the "current" value function, since the flows of utility from consumption services are also discounted back to time $t = 0$. The stochastic Bellman equation for this control problem is

$$\rho V(W) = \max_{c,\omega's}\left\{\frac{1}{\gamma}S(W)^{\gamma} + W\mu_w V'(W) + \frac{1}{2}W^2\sigma_w^2 V''(W)\right\},$$

where μ_w has already been defined, and

$$\sigma_W^2 = \omega_K^2 \sigma_K^2 + (\omega_M + \omega_B)^2 \sigma_\Pi^2 + (\omega_{M^*} + \omega_{B^*})^2 \sigma_{\Pi^*}^2 + 2\omega_K (\omega_M + \omega_B) \sigma_{K\Pi}$$
$$+ 2\omega_K (\omega_{M^*} + \omega_{B^*}) \sigma_{K\Pi^*} + 2(\omega_M + \omega_B)(\omega_{M^*} + \omega_{B^*}) \sigma_{\Pi\Pi^*}$$

The symbols $\sigma_{K\Pi}$, $\sigma_{K\Pi^*}$ and $\sigma_{\Pi\Pi^*}$ are defined as follows:

$$\sigma_{K\Pi} \equiv cov(K, \Pi) \equiv \sigma_K \sigma_\Pi \rho_{K\Pi} \equiv \sigma_K \sigma_\Pi E(dz_K dz_\Pi),$$

$$\sigma_{K\Pi^*} \equiv cov(K, \Pi^*) \equiv \sigma_K \sigma_{\Pi^*} \rho_{K\Pi^*} \equiv \sigma_K \sigma_{\Pi^*} E(dz_K dz_{\Pi^*}), \text{ and}$$

$$\sigma_{\Pi\Pi^*} \equiv cov(\Pi, \Pi^*) \equiv \sigma_\Pi \sigma_{\Pi^*} \rho_{\Pi\Pi^*} \equiv \sigma_\Pi \sigma_{\Pi^*} E(dz_\Pi dz_{\Pi^*}).$$

There are six optimality conditions: one for c and one for each portfolio share. Each optimality condition takes the following form, where x is any of the control variables, and the indicated partial derivatives may easily be computed, using the definitions of $S(W)$, μ_W, and σ_W^2:

$$S^{\gamma-1} \frac{\partial S}{\partial x} + WV'(W) \frac{\partial \mu_W}{\partial x} + \frac{1}{2} W^2 V''(W) \frac{\partial \sigma_W^2}{\partial x}.$$

Exercise 15.4

The restrictions imposed on the model developed in exercises 15.2 and 15.3 are sufficient to permit one to derive a complete analytical solution for each of the control variables. You may want to find these reduced form solutions for something fun to do. In this exercise, however, the objective is simply to proceed far enough into the problem, that a solution strategy becomes apparent.

First, use the optimality conditions corresponding to the choices of ω_K, ω_B and ω_{B^*} to derive a set of linear relationships between the expected excess returns on those assets and the portfolio shares ω_K, $(\omega_M + \omega_B)$ and $(\omega_{M^*} + \omega_{B^*})$. Next, use the optimality conditions for ω_M and ω_{M^*} to derive a reduced form expression for the ratio:

$$\left[\frac{\omega_M}{\omega_{M^*}}\right] \equiv \left[\frac{\Pi M}{\Pi^* M^*}\right].$$

Can you see a path to the solution?

Hint: It turns out that the value function must be of the form $V(W) = AW^\gamma$, where A is an undetermined coefficient. This form can be used to simplify the expressions you derive in this exercise.

Solution: The optimality conditions for ω_K, ω_B and ω_{B^*} do not involve S, and using the fact (given the form we postulated for $V(W)$), that

$$-\frac{WV''(W)}{V'(W)} = 1 - \gamma,$$

these conditions simplify to:

$$\mu_K - r = (1-\gamma)\left[\omega_K \sigma_K^2 + (\omega_M + \omega_B)\sigma_{K\Pi} + (\omega_{M^*} + \omega_{B^*})\sigma_{K\Pi^*}\right],$$

$$R + \mu_\Pi - r = (1-\gamma)\left[(\omega_M + \omega_B)\sigma_\Pi^2 + \omega_K \sigma_{K\Pi} + (\omega_{M^*} + \omega_{B^*})\sigma_{\Pi\Pi^*}\right], \text{ and}$$

$$R^* + \mu_{\Pi^*} - r = (1-\gamma)\left[(\omega_{M^*} + \omega_{B^*})\sigma_{\Pi^*}^2 + \omega_K \sigma_{K\Pi^*} + (\omega_M + \omega_B)\sigma_{\Pi\Pi^*}\right].$$

Now form a ratio from the optimality conditions for domestic and foreign real balances and calculate:

$$\frac{\partial S/\partial \omega_M}{\partial S/\partial \omega_{M^*}} = \frac{a}{1-a}\left[\frac{\omega_M}{\omega_{M^*}}\right]^{\beta-1}.$$

We can now write the following expressions involving the ratio of domestic to foreign real balances:

$$\left[\frac{\omega_M}{\omega_{M^*}}\right]^{\beta-1} = \frac{\dfrac{V'(W)}{WV''(W)}\dfrac{\partial \mu_W}{\partial \omega_M} + \dfrac{1}{2}\dfrac{\partial \sigma_W^2}{\partial \omega_M}}{\dfrac{V'(W)}{WV''(W)}\dfrac{\partial \mu_W}{\partial \omega_{M^*}} + \dfrac{1}{2}\dfrac{\partial \sigma_W^2}{\partial \omega_{M^*}}} \cdot \frac{1-a}{a}.$$

Use the optimality conditions for capital and bonds to simplify this relationship to the following equation:

$$\frac{\omega_M}{\omega_{M^*}} \equiv \frac{\Pi M}{\Pi^* M^*} = \left[\frac{aR^*}{(1-a)R}\right]^{\frac{1}{1-\beta}}.$$

Finally, we would compute the expressions for

$$\frac{\partial S/\partial \omega_M}{\partial S/\partial c} \text{ and } \frac{\partial S/\partial \omega_{M^*}}{\partial S/\partial c},$$

and utilize them in ratios formed from the optimality conditions for domestic money and consumption and, respectively, from the optimality conditions for foreign money and consumption. Now we have six equations for the six control variables. After solving for reduced forms, substitute the results into the stochastic Bellman equation to solve for the coefficient A, thereby determining the current value function.

Exercise 15.5

Provide an intuitive interpretation of the results derived in Exercise 15.4. Although we have not really laid the groundwork to extend the model to general equilibrium, it is not too much of a stretch to assume that the optimality conditions derived in Exercise 15.3 reflect the preferences of a representative agent, and also to assume that similar conditions apply to the representative agent of a foreign country (allowing for possible differences in preference parameters). Suppose further that purchasing power parity holds at all times. Letting e denote the nominal exchange rate, we assume that $\Pi^* = e\Pi \quad \forall\, t$. Discuss the implications of the results derived in Exercise 15.4 for the determination of the exchange rate in this economy.

Hint: Think about the way in which preferences with respect to risk and intertemporal substitution impact various portfolio allocation decisions made by the investor.

Solution: The first intermediate result derived in Exercise 15.4 can easily be solved for ω_K, $(\omega_M + \omega_B)$ and $(\omega_{M^*} + \omega_{B^*})$. Using linear algebra notation, we find that

$$\begin{bmatrix} \omega_K \\ \omega_M + \omega_B \\ \omega_{M^*} + \omega_{B^*} \end{bmatrix} = \frac{1}{1-\gamma} \begin{bmatrix} \sigma_K^2 & \sigma_{K\Pi} & \sigma_{K\Pi^*} \\ \sigma_{K\Pi} & \sigma_\Pi^2 & \sigma_{\Pi\Pi^*} \\ \sigma_{K\Pi^*} & \sigma_{\Pi\Pi^*} & \sigma_{\Pi^*}^2 \end{bmatrix}^{-1} \begin{bmatrix} \mu_K - r \\ R + \mu_\Pi - r \\ R^* + \mu_{\Pi^*} - r \end{bmatrix}.$$

The implication of this result is that a portion of the asset allocation decision can be made independently of the optimal consumption / savings decision.

Specifically, the investor can divide his wealth into three asset categories: capital, domestic assets and foreign assets.

The second intermediate result suggests that, taking R and R^* as given, risk does not impact the allocation of total money balances between domestic and foreign currency. This result reflects that fact that any purchasing power risk associated with holding a given currency may be perfectly hedged by taking an offsetting position in bonds denominated in that currency.

Finally, by combining the definition of purchasing power parity with the second intermediate result from Exercise 15.4, we find that:

$$e = \frac{M^S}{M^{*S}} \left[\frac{(1-a)R}{aR^*} \right]^{\frac{1}{1-\beta}}.$$

The S superscripts denote the supply of money, which must equal the desired holdings of money in general equilibrium. Stulz imposes market clearing conditions and derives general equilibrium expressions for R, R^* and e. He shows that the instantaneous covariances between the rate of change of the purchasing power of each currency and the rate of consumption growth are the only channels by which risk affects nominal bond yields and the nominal exchange rate.

Exercise 15.6

Robert Lucas analyzed the asset pricing implications of a two-country, discrete time, cash-in-advance model, in which the representative agent in each country chooses consumption and portfolio asset shares so as to maximize expected lifetime utility over an infinite horizon (1982, *Journal of Monetary Economics*, 10, 335-360). The objective of the representative agent is to

$$\max \quad E_0 \left[\sum_{t=0}^{\infty} \beta^t u(C_t^0, C_t^1) \right] \quad ; \quad 0 < \beta < 1$$

s.t.
$$W_{t+1} = \frac{1}{P_{t+1}^0} \left[m_t^0 - P_t^0 C_t^0 + e_{t+1}(m_t^1 - P_t^1 C_t^1) \right] + r_{t+1}^0 \psi_t^0 + r_{t+1}^1 \psi_t^1$$

$$+ \psi_t^0 \frac{\omega_{t+1}^0 M_t^0}{P_{t+1}^0} + \psi_t^1 \frac{e_{t+1} \omega_{t+1}^1 M_t^1}{P_{t+1}^0} + q_{t+1}^0 \theta_t^0 + q_{t+1}^1 \theta_t^1$$

$$+ \theta_t^0 \frac{P_t^0 \varepsilon_t^0}{P_{t+1}^0} + \theta_t^1 \frac{e_{t+1} P_t^1 \varepsilon_t^1}{P_{t+1}^0},$$

$$P_t^0 C_t^0 \leq m_t^0, \text{ and } P_t^1 C_t^1 \leq m_t^1.$$

The inequalities are cash-in-advance constraints, which will hold as equalities, given the usual assumptions regarding the shape of the felicity function. Superscripts denote the country, while time subscript conventions are chosen such that variables with a t subscript are known at the start of time t. There are two consumption goods, with the output of good i occurring only in county i (i=0,1) according to an exogenous stochastic process. However, agents in each country may trade internationally, allowing them the option to consume both goods. There are four assets, which may also be traded internationally: claims to output streams for goods 0 and 1, and claims to monetary transfers for each country's currency. Each agent is initially endowed with a claim to his home country's output process and a claim to a stream of home country currency transfers. We assume that the total value of initial endowments is the same for each agent, and everyone has the same preferences. Unfortunately, there is a good deal of notation to keep track of, and it is defined as follows.

ψ_t^i	$\equiv$	number of claims to currency i transfers held at time t
θ_t^i	$\equiv$	number of claims to good i output streams held at time t
C_t^i	$\equiv$	consumption of good i during period t
P_t^i	$\equiv$	price of good i in the currency of country i at time t
r_t^i	$\equiv$	price of claims to currency i transfers in units of good 0
q_t^i	$\equiv$	good 0 price of claims to country i output streams
e_t	$\equiv$	exchange rate in units of currency 0 per unit of currency 1
M_t^i	$\equiv$	currency transfers per claim at time t
m_t^i	$\equiv$	desired holdings of currency i at time t
ω_t^i	$\equiv$	random growth rate of currency i transfers per claim at time t
ε_t^i	$\equiv$	randomly determined output of good i per claim at time t
W_t	$\equiv$	real (good 0) wealth of the agent at the start of period t

We should emphasize that ψ_t^i, θ_t^i, C_t^i, m_t^i, and W_t are quantities for one representative agent. It doesn't matter which one, since the equilibrium we will look at is symmetric with respect to the two countries.

Solve the representative agent's optimization problem, and derive a general Euler equation that could be used to price any asset in this economy. You may assume that all exogenous random variables follow first order Markov processes.

Hint: The flow wealth constraint simplifies when you impose the cash-in-advance constraints as equalities. Currency holdings cease to be a choice variable when these restrictions are imposed.

Solution: Taking the above hint into account, we can write the optimization problem as follows: choose C_t^0, C_t^1, ψ_t^0, ψ_t^1, θ_t^0, and θ_t^1 for each time period so as to:

$$\max \quad E_t\left[\sum_{j=0}^{\infty}\beta^j u\left(C_{t+j}^0, C_{t+j}^1\right)\right]$$

s.t. $W_t = C_t^0 + \dfrac{e_t P_t^1 C_t^1}{P_t^0} + r_t^0\psi_t^0 + r_t^1\psi_t^1 + q_t^0\theta_t^0 + q_t^1\theta_t^1$, and

$$W_{t+1} = \theta_t^0\left[q_{t+1}^0 + \frac{P_t^0\varepsilon_t^0}{P_{t+1}^0}\right] + \theta_t^1\left[q_{t+1}^1 + \frac{e_{t+1}P_t^1\varepsilon_t^1}{P_{t+1}^0}\right]$$
$$+ \psi_t^0\left[r_{t+1}^0 + \frac{\omega_{t+1}^0 M_t^0}{P_{t+1}^0}\right] + \psi_t^1\left[r_{t+1}^1 + \frac{e_{t+1}\omega_{t+1}^1 M_t^1}{P_{t+1}^0}\right].$$

The necessary conditions for an optimum include the wealth constraints shown above, as well as the static optimality condition

$$\frac{u_0\left(C_t^0, C_t^1\right)}{u_1\left(C_t^0, C_t^1\right)} = \frac{P_t^0}{e_t P_t^1},$$

and an Euler equation for each of the four assets of the form

$$u_0\left(C_t^0, C_t^1\right) = \beta E_t\left[\left(1+\rho_{t+1}\right)u_0\left(C_{t+1}^0, C_{t+1}^1\right)\right],$$

where ρ_{t+1} denotes the net return on a given asset in terms of good 0. For example, the net return on a claim to currency 0 monetary transfers is given by

$$\rho_{t+1} = \frac{r_{t+1}^0 + \dfrac{\omega_{t+1}^0 M_t^0}{P_{t+1}^0}}{r_t^0} - 1.$$

The time subscript denotes the time when the return on a claim purchased in the previous period will be realized.

Exercise 15.7

This exercise continues the analysis begun in exercise 15.6. Impose goods and money market clearing conditions, and derive general equilibrium expressions for P_t^0 and P_t^1 and for the exchange rate e_t. Using the appropriate form of the Euler equation, and assuming that covered interest parity holds:

$$F_t = \frac{1+i_{t+1}}{1+i_{t+1}^*}e_t,$$

derive a general equilibrium expression for the one period forward exchange rate, F_t. Note that i_{t+1} (the domestic nominal interest rate) and i_{t+1}^* (the foreign nominal interest rate) are known with certainty at time t. The real returns on one period bonds are not known at time t, however, since goods prices are random.

Hint: There is a complete set of asset markets in this economy (i.e. one for each source of randomness), allowing each agent to eliminate all idiosyncratic risk through diversification.

Solution: Because asset markets are already complete, bonds will be priced such that they are not traded in equilibrium. In addition, given that all agents have identical preferences and begin with the same initial wealth, it must be the case that each person holds the same portfolio and consumes the same mix of goods each period. Thus, the market clearing conditions are particularly simple:

$$C_t^0 = \frac{1}{2}\varepsilon_t^0, \quad C_t^1 = \frac{1}{2}\varepsilon_t^1, \quad m_t^0 = \frac{1}{2}M_t^0, \text{ and } m_t^1 = \frac{1}{2}M_t^1.$$

Using the cash-in advance constraints, which we know must bind at the optimum, we can derive general equilibrium expressions for goods prices:

$$P_t^0 = \frac{M_t^0}{\varepsilon_t^0}, \text{ and } P_t^1 = \frac{M_t^1}{\varepsilon_t^1}.$$

Now use the static optimality condition to solve for the nominal exchange rate in general equilibrium:

$$e_t = \frac{\left(\dfrac{M_t^0}{\varepsilon_t^0}\right) u_1\left(\dfrac{1}{2}\varepsilon_t^0, \dfrac{1}{2}\varepsilon_t^1\right)}{\left(\dfrac{M_t^1}{\varepsilon_t^1}\right) u_0\left(\dfrac{1}{2}\varepsilon_t^0, \dfrac{1}{2}\varepsilon_t^1\right)}.$$

In order to derive a general equilibrium expression for F_t, we use the standard Euler equation to implicitly determine i_t and i_t^*. Doing this for each asset and equating the two optimality expressions for $u_0(C_t^0, C_t^1)$, we determine the following asset pricing relationship:

$$E_t\left[\frac{(1+i_{t+1})}{(P_{t+1}^0/P_t^0)} u_0(C_{t+1}^0, C_{t+1}^1)\right] = E_t\left[\frac{(1+i_{t+1}^*)(e_{t+1}/e_t)}{(P_{t+1}^0/P_t^0)} u_0(C_{t+1}^0, C_{t+1}^1)\right].$$

Multiply through by $\dfrac{e_t}{P_t^0(1+i_t^*)}$ and make use of the covered interest parity relationship to derive the following expression for the forward rate:

$$F_t = \frac{E_t\left[\dfrac{e_{t+1} u_0(C_{t+1}^0, C_{t+1}^1)}{P_{t+1}^0}\right]}{E_t\left[\dfrac{u_0(C_{t+1}^0, C_{t+1}^1)}{P_{t+1}^0}\right]}.$$